When we pray...

When we pray...

Meditation on the Lord's Prayer

Eugene LaVerdiere, sss

AVE MARIA PRESS   Notre Dame, Indiana

Acknowledgments:

Unless otherwise noted, the scripture texts used in this work have been translated by the author.

The Lord's Prayer, Luke 11:2-4, page 166:

from the NEW AMERICAN BIBLE, copyright © 1970, by the Confraternity of Christian Doctrine, Washington, D.C., is used by permission of copyright owner. All rights reserved.

from THE JERUSALEM BIBLE, copyright © 1966 by Darton, Longman & Todd, Ltd. and Doubleday & Company, Inc. Used by permission of the publisher.

from THE NEW ENGLISH BIBLE, copyright © 1961, 1970 by the Delegates of the Oxford University Press and the Syndics of the Cambridge University Press.

from the REVISED STANDARD VERSION, copyright © 1973 by Division of Christian Education of the National Council of the Churches of Christ in the United States of America. All rights reserved.

International Standard Book Number: 0-87793-262-X (Cloth)
0-87793-263-8 (Paper)

Library of Congress Catalog Card Number: 82-73512

Printed and bound in the United States of America.

Cover design: Elizabeth French

To my brother Gary

Many have undertaken to interpret the prayer which the Lord himself taught us, just as it was transmitted to us by the ministers of the word who first heard and prayed it. I too have carefully traced the course of its tradition from the beginning and have decided to present my interpretation in writing for you, so that, aware of your Christian dignity, you may come to pray the prayer which you once recited.

Paraphrase of Luke 1:1-4

Contents

Preface

The Lord's Prayer that we recite so frequently is derived from St. Matthew. Routine repetitions often serve to deaden our appreciation of everything that this prayer implies. Like the Good News of Christ, which we have in four separate interpretations, St. Luke's version of the Lord's Prayer differs somewhat from Matthew's. In many ways closer to the original given by Jesus, it helps us to appreciate both the prayer's uniqueness and its centrality in Christian life.

Father Eugene LaVerdiere has plunged boldly ahead and offers us a profound interpretation of Luke's prayer in the context of Luke's own theology. He does this so that we can pray it today with the depth of understanding enjoyed by the Lukan community, allowing it to challenge us to exercise like responsibility for building Christ's kingdom.

Each phrase is carefully analyzed. Its implications then and now are disengaged. And each chapter ends in a prayer arising from the text.

It may be asked whether all the exegetical work is necessary to arrive at the practical prayer section that ends each chapter. The answer is most definitely yes, for the dust of centuries must be removed in order for us to appreciate the riches that lie beneath.

In actual fact, the work is both exciting and rewarding. In no other way can we gain those insights into each phrase and into the prayer as a whole that enable us to see just how the Lord's Prayer is absolutely central to Luke's entire gospel. Most gospel commentaries focus on individual passages. LaVerdiere enables us to understand the Lord's Prayer as that key which unlocks the rich vision Luke possessed of Christ's life and how we are all caught up in the same mission. It is the Father who has graced us for this journey, strengthening us each day with our eucharistic bread.

—Paul Bernier, sss

Introduction

"The interpreter of the scriptures is like the director of an orchestra." This comparison, which a friend recently shared in conversation, began as a simple observation. But then, aware that he had my attention, he continued: "Exegetes explain the text, unveil its meaning, and hold up its values, but they also express it creatively. They bring us to experience the Word and to live the gospel. The interpreter is a witness to the gospel." The simple observation had developed into an extremely demanding challenge. It spoke far more of hope, of what interpretation ought to be, than of fact, of what it most often is.

In this book, which deals with the Lukan tradition and interpretation of the Lord's Prayer, I try to meet that challenge. My purpose is to explain the text, bring out its meaning, and help my fellow Christians to experience it in prayer.

Text

The Lord's Prayer according to Luke (11:2-4) is a simple prayer, shorter than the Lord's Prayer according to Matthew (6:9-13) and unique in some of its wording. Comparisons between the two texts will help us to recognize the distinctive features of the Lukan text and see how it witnessed to a very ancient tradition. The main effort, however,

13

will be to interpret the prayer precisely as it stands in Luke's gospel.

Scholars have often examined the prayer in its most primitive setting and tried to uncover its oldest form and meaning within the teaching of Jesus. They have also investigated the development of its tradition and the two forms of that tradition which were inherited by Matthew and Luke. Those who have studied it in its gospel setting have usually focused on Matthew's text and interpreted it in the light of Matthew's gospel. For the most part Luke's text has been treated in relation to Matthew, and apart from commentaries, there has been little effort to present the Lord's Prayer as an integral part of Luke's gospel.

Explaining the text of the Lord's Prayer according to Luke is a fourfold effort. First, it requires concentration on the text. Second, it means exploring the text's language from the standpoint of language usage in Luke-Acts. Third, it calls for examining the prayer's literary function within the overall pastoral and historical statement of Luke-Acts. And fourth, it invites seeing Luke-Acts and special sections of it as a Lukan commentary on the tradition of the Lord's Prayer which he and his communities had inherited.

In taking up an old tradition Luke did not necessarily use its language as it had been used outside of his gospel synthesis. In New Testament times, as today, the words *Father, name, kingdom, bread, sins* and *test* implied different things for different people. To uncover the prayer's special Lukan nuances, Luke-Acts itself is our primary and most authoritative commentary. All others are secondary.

Meaning

The text of Luke's Lord's Prayer is a meaningful text. It overflowed with meaning when the early Christians first heard and shared it, and when the gospel writers wrote it down. It has had meaning throughout the Christian centuries, and it has meaning today.

To say that a text has meaning is to say that it has reference points outside of itself in the life of those who read it and speak it. For the Lord's Prayer, some of these reference points are related to special prayer contexts. The Lord's Prayer may be associated with moments at a parent's knee, with a conversion experience or with repeated liturgical experiences. Other reference points are more general and have nothing to do with prayer, as when the word *father* draws meaning from the experience of having a father, or of not knowing one's father, or of being a father. Finding meaning in a text is connecting that text with a whole complex of such experiences.

In light of these considerations the text's meaning cannot be restricted to what the author intended or how his first readers grasped it. It has to include reference points in the lives of all who continue to read it. Otherwise, we would have to say that the text may once have been meaningful, but that it is now meaningless. The love and respect which all Christians have for the Lord's Prayer show that it is certainly not meaningless. On the contrary, it is a classical Christian prayer, open to multiple experiences of what it expresses, inexhaustible. There are other classics of Christian prayer, but the Lord's Prayer is in a category by itself. As the *Lord's* prayer, it is the normative Christian prayer against which every other prayer, including the classics, is measured and evaluated.

In bringing out the prayer's meaning we shall approach it as part of a continuous conversation or dialectic between the meaning it had in the gospel and the meaning it has today. Our experience helps us to see what the prayer meant. In turn, what it meant helps us to see both what it actually means and what it could mean for us.

Experience

The interpreter's task does not end with explaining the text and its background, nor with drawing out the text's meaning for Christian living today. All of this is but a preparation for the experience of prayer. But how does the interpreter facilitate the experience of prayer, an experience which shapes life and discloses the prayer's meaning in a way which mere explanations can only betray?

From the viewpoint of the writer's experience, having

prayed the Lord's Prayer is indispensable. Only then will writing have the inspirational quality needed to communicate the inspired word. This realization calls for humility, for the ability to recognize and accept one's limitations in praying the Lord's Prayer and in praying it according to Luke.

A comprehensive effort to witness to the Lukan tradition of the Lord's Prayer is necessarily limited or enhanced by the interpreter's knowledge of the text, grasp of its meaning, and experience of prayer. Consequently, like a good orchestra director, the interpreter provides not *the* interpretation but *an* interpretation of the Lord's Prayer. With this awareness, the interpreter's hope is that his or her intelligence, experience, diligence, imagination and creative abilities will provide an interpretation which is of Christian value to others. Such is my prayer.

*   *   *   *

In writing this book I am indebted to the scholars of many nations who have greatly contributed to our modern understanding of the Lord's Prayer. I have attempted, however, to go beyond their work and to interpret the prayer afresh in light of the growing awareness that understanding the history and meaning of the text is not enough.

I am particularly indebted to those who insist that "the interpreter is a witness to the gospel," to the members of my Blessed Sacrament community, to the faculty, students and staff of Catholic Theological Union in Chicago who daily prod me to provide that witness, and to Frank Cunningham, Joan Bellina and Kenneth Peters, my editors at Ave Maria Press, who helped me translate it into this book.

My greatest debt, however, is to those who acted in the Lord's name and taught me how to pray the Lord's Prayer. First, there were my parents, with whom I stumbled through the Lord's Prayer as soon as words started to form on my lips. In recent years there has been the liturgical experience of singing the Lord's Prayer in the Eucharist at Santa Cruz Church in Manila. It is there that for the first time I realized how true it is that the Lord's Prayer is a classical prayer and that it transcends all cultures and social contexts. Closer to home, there has been the liturgy at St. Paschal Baylon Church in Cleveland, where the Lord's Prayer wells up from the assembly as from one voice. Hands joined, the assembly smiles its song. Full-throated, it sings its peace.

My brother Gary, a Brother in the Congregation of the Blessed Sacrament, is the liturgical coordinator at St. Paschal's, and this book is dedicated to him in gratitude for that experience of the Lord's Prayer.

—Eugene A. LaVerdiere, sss

Part I

Preparation

One

In an extremely old Christian creed we are told that "Christ died for our sins *according to the scriptures*" and that "he rose on the third day *according to the scriptures*" (1 Cor 15:3-5). The creed testifies to the fact that from the beginning the early Christians formulated their faith according to the scriptures, much like the synagogue Jews among whom they lived.

The expression "according to the scriptures" spoke the Christians' conviction that their faith was indeed in fulfillment of the scriptures, and it spelled out a method of reflection on Christian events along with a creative way of articulating those events with scriptural language. Every book in the New Testament, from Matthew's gospel to the Book of Revelation, illustrates this triple significance of the expression "according to the scriptures."

In this book, which is about praying the Lord's Prayer according to one work in the New Testament scriptures, Luke-Acts, we want to speak our prayer in faith according to Luke, reflect on it in a Lukan way and articulate our reflection with the help of Lukan language. To do so, we must become thoroughly familiar with the prayer's Lukan context. In this first chapter our focus is on the literary context.

First, we shall explore the prayer's immediate context in Luke 11:1-3. This will help us to dissociate it from the

21

Matthean context with which most Christians are far more familiar. In Matthew the Lord's Prayer (6:9-13) appears in the sermon or discourse on the mount (Mt 5-7) along with other instructions on giving alms, prayer and fasting.

Second, we shall situate the prayer in Luke's great journey narrative (9:51-24:53) and show how, in many respects, this narrative comments on the Lord's Prayer.

Context in Luke 11:1-13

In Luke, the Lord's Prayer is found in a short passage which is entirely devoted to the subject of prayer (11:1-13). This passage includes three sections: verse 1, verses 2-4, and verses 5-13.

First we have an introduction (11:1) which situates Jesus' teaching with regard to time, place, what Jesus was doing on the occasion, and who was present. Within this setting, the narrator introduces a request made by one of the disciples.

The many elements in this introductory verse are most easily seen when we outline it in sense lines.

> Once when he was praying in a certain place,
> just as he finished,
> one of his disciples said to him,
>> "Lord,
>> teach us to pray,
>> as John taught his disciples."

We shall analyze this verse at great length in Chapters Two and Three from the point of view of the nature of the one who made the request and from that of the experience which gave rise to it. At this point it suffices to establish the verse's literary function as an introduction.

But what does verse 1 introduce? The tendency is to answer, "The Lord's Prayer, of course." This answer is not wrong, but it falls short of the narrator's intent. In the verses which follow, Jesus does fulfill the disciple's request with the Lord's Prayer (11:2-4). But the disciples must know far more than the Lord's Prayer. Accordingly, Jesus goes on to teach them about the need to persevere in praying that prayer and about the certitude and quality of their Father's response (11:5-13). Jesus' response to the disciple's request includes *both* verses 2-4 and verses 5-13.

The second section in the passage, then, is the Lord's Prayer itself (11:2-4). Like the disciple's request, it has a few words of introduction, some of which belong to the narrator and some of which are attributed to Jesus, who has just been addressed as Lord.

> He said to them,
>> "When you pray, say:
>>> 'Father,
>>>> hallowed be your name.
>>>> Your kingdom come.
>>>> Give us each day our daily bread;
>>>> and forgive us our sins
>>>>> even as we ourselves forgive
>>>>> everyone who is indebted to us;
>>>> and do not bring us to the test.' "

As we see from the prayer's immediate introduction (11:2a), the prayer is explicitly given as the second part of a brief dialogue between a disciple and Jesus, the Lord. In his answer, however, the Lord does not speak to that disciple alone, but to all the disciples. This procedure is not unusual in Luke's gospel. Recall how on the road to Emmaus a disciple named Cleopas spoke to Jesus, and how Jesus responded to both of the disciples whom he accompanied on the journey. In such cases the one disciple speaks for the others, and it is only appropriate that Jesus should address his answer to all. We shall study the text of the Lord's Prayer in Chapter Four. Detailed material on the text is also provided in the Appendix.

As already stated, the passage's third section (11:5-13) contains further teaching.

> And he said to them,
>> "Which of you who has a friend . . ."

This section is linked to what precedes by the "and," but it is also separated from the prayer by the repetition of "he said to them" (verse 5). In 11:2-4 Jesus taught a prayer. In 11:5-13 he teaches a number of things about praying.

After the opening statement, which attributes the teaching to Jesus, there is a brief discourse composed of different kinds of teaching and whose origins in Jesus' setting were quite varied. In keeping with the contemporary norms for historical writing, Jesus' discourse is a Lukan composition which drew distinct traditions into a synthesis and presented them as spoken on one occasion. This allowed Luke to gather a number of parables and sayings of Jesus and show their relationship to the Lord's Prayer.

This third section begins with a parable about a man who asks a friend for bread that he might extend proper hospitality to another friend who has arrived from a journey in the middle of the night (11:5-7). Jesus then reflects on an aspect of this parable: He shows how the man's persistence was rewarded (verse 8). The parable's context (11:1-13) relates it to the petition for our daily bread. Its purpose, however, is not so much to develop the nature of that petition as to emphasize how the disciples must persevere in praying it.

On the basis of his reflection, Jesus then presents a general principle for his disciples (verse 9). This principle, which begins with "Ask, and you shall receive," is directly applied to those present, as we see from the pronoun "you" and the second person plural of the verbs in the Greek text. The principle's triple form, with its careful balance of verbs and use of pronouns, indicates that it must have played an important role in spoken tradition. A literal translation brings out this balance:

Ask
        and it shall be given to you;
seek
        and you shall find;
knock
        and it shall be opened to you.

In early Christian life this saying of Jesus' could be applied to various contexts. In a different form it appears in Mark 11:24 where it refers explicitly to prayer:

> Therefore I tell you,
> > whatever you ask in prayer,
> > believe that you have received it,
> > and it shall be yours.

In this Markan context, emphasis is not so much on asking as on what is asked, "whatever you ask," and on the conditions for receiving it, "believe that you have received it."

The principle is also found in Matthew's sermon on the mount (7:7), in a wording identical to that of Luke, but not in the part of the sermon which deals with prayer (6:5-15).

After addressing the saying directly to the disciples, Luke immediately presents it in another form (11:10):

> Everyone who asks
> > receives,
> and one who seeks
> > finds,
> and to one who knocks,
> > it is opened.

The second saying's structure is obviously quite different from the first. From the use of the same verbs, however, we see that it constituted a distinct development of the same traditional saying. Its most distinctive feature lies in the universal application, "*Everyone* who asks." The second person plural which gave the first saying such immediacy is gone.

In the Lukan text we thus pass from an application to the disciples who were present to a universal statement concerning everyone who prays. Jesus' discourse consequently moves beyond the original setting of the first disciples to address all future readers of Luke's gospel. The same phenomenon is found in Matthew, who also used the general "everyone" form of the saying immediately after the "you" form (Mt 7:8). Again the wording in Matthew and Luke is identical, with one exception: Matthew has the concluding verb in the future, "it will be opened"; Luke has it in the present, "it is opened." For Luke the Lord's Prayer is answered in the very moment when we pray it.

The final part of the passage on prayer is the parable about how a father's response does not betray a son's trust but corresponds to the request which he has made.

> What father among you, if his son asks for a fish, will instead of a fish give him a serpent; or if he asks for an egg, will give him a scorpion? If you then, who are evil, know how to give good gifts to your children, how much more will the heavenly Father give the Holy Spirit to those who ask him! (Lk 11:11-13, *RSV*)

What applies to the human order applies to the divine order *a fortiori*.

Like the first parable (11:5-7), which began with "Which of *you*," the concluding parable draws the disciples and the readers directly into the parable, "What father among *you*." Enjoying the immediacy of the first saying, "Ask and it shall be given to *you*," both parables involve Jesus' listeners as participants in the parable. Instead of telling a story about someone else who models the disciples' lives, Jesus tells two stories about typical situations in the lives of the disciples themselves. The difference is striking. In most parables the disciples are expected to identify with those who play a role in the story. In Luke 11:5-7 and 11:13 they are expected to recognize how they themselves would behave or not behave in hypothetical situations.

In Matthew, the same parable is found immediately after the two sayings on asking and receiving (7:7-8). Again the Matthean and Lukan forms are nearly identical, but with a glaring difference. In Matthew, the heavenly Father is expected to give "good things" to anyone who asks him (7:11). In Luke, the heavenly Father gives "the Holy Spirit" (11:13). The Lord's Prayer—its address to the Father and all of its petitions—is consequently summarized in the gift of the Holy Spirit, the creative source of life and the energizing power of the Christian mission. After assuring the disciples that the Father rewards persistent prayer according to their needs (11:8), Luke identifies those needs. The Lord's Prayer is a prayer for the Holy Spirit.

Context in Luke 9:51-24:53

The Lord's Prayer and the short teaching passage in which it appears are part of a long journey narrative whose scope and nature are explicitly indicated in the journey's opening verse, "When the days drew near for him to be received up, he set his face to go to Jerusalem" (9:51, *RSV*). The journey is to Jerusalem, where the gospel story began and where it would end. Jerusalem, however, is not merely the journey's geographical destination or even the city of the passion-resurrection. It is the place of the ascension, Jesus' entry into the glory of his Father's heavenly home.

The earthly symbol for the Father's home is Jerusalem's Temple. Hence the gospel's focus on the Temple in the annunciation of the conception and birth of John the Baptist (1:5-22), in the finding of Jesus on the third day (2:46), in Jesus' entry into Jerusalem (19:45), and in the ascension itself (24:52-53).

The Lord's Prayer is thus part of Jesus' journey to the Father, a journey in which he is accompanied by the disciples. This larger context (9:51-24:53) shows that Luke saw the Lord's Prayer as the prayer of the Christian journey. From the journey's description in the transfiguration scene, it can also be called the prayer of the Christian exodus (9:31).

Luke's emphasis on the journey's destination, Jerusalem, the Temple, the Father's heavenly dwelling, indicates that it is indeed an eschatological prayer, one which looks to the consummation of history and the fullness of God's reign. But as a prayer for Christians who are on the way, it also addresses the daily needs of those who already have been blessed with the presence of the kingdom.

Within the journey narrative the prayer passage (11:1-13) immediately follows the story of Martha and Mary, and together with that little account opens the body (10:38-13:21) of the journey narrative's first section (9:51-13:21). Attention to the Lord and listening to his word is the one thing needed, the absolutely fundamental attitude, and the Lord's Prayer is the one prayer needed, the elemental prayer, for the Christian journey to the Father.

The journey's long introduction (9:51-10:37) presents it as a missionary journey. This too helps us to grasp the nature of the Lord's Prayer. From the very beginning Jesus sent his disciples as messengers ahead of him to prepare the Lord's advent (9:51-56). In their mission they were joined by others who accepted the invitation to follow Jesus as the Son of Man and Lord. As their numbers swelled, the Lord appointed an additional seventy-two whom he sent in pairs to every town and place he was to visit. In their mission the hopes of prophets and kings were fulfilled thanks to the Father who was revealed to them in the Son. The Lord's Prayer is thus the prayer of the Christian missionary journey, a prayer to be uttered in full assurance of the Father's presence and of the mission's success. It is the prayer of those who see and hear what prophets and kings for centuries had longed to see and hear, the prayer of those whose eyes have been blest with the Son's own vision.

One of the important themes in the journey's introduction is the disciples' reaction to the Samaritan rejection of their mission (9:52-55). Confronted by this rejection, James and John want to call down fire from heaven to destroy the Samaritans. This reaction is most inappropriate, and the Lord reprimands them. The reason for this becomes clear a little later when Jesus answers a lawyer's self-justifying question with the story of the good Samaritan (10:25-37). In this final unit of the introduction the lawyer is skillfully led to recognize his neighbor in one who normally would not have been accepted as a neighbor. But even more skillfully Jesus shows the lawyer that he should not be concerned about who his neighbor is. Rather, he should concentrate on being a good neighbor to others, as good a neighbor as the Samaritan who cared for the hapless victim by the wayside.

The Samaritan theme introduces one of the fundamental attitudes of those who pray the prayer of the Christian missionary journey, an open and forgiving attitude for all (11:4). The Lord's Prayer is not the prayer of those who distinguish those who are their neighbor from those who are not. It is the prayer of the Christian neighbor to all.

The first part of the journey (9:51-13:21) develops many other aspects of the disciples' attitude at prayer. They must be confident that the Holy Spirit will teach them what to say when they are persecuted. Like Jesus they are not to set themselves up as judge over others. The Lord's Prayer is not a judgmental prayer. Even as they ask for nourishment and all that is essential for living, they are not to be anxious. They must pray with full confidence that the Father will provide for them. They must seek the Father's reign over them, a reign which has already been given them, which is even now in their midst, but which is like a tiny mustard seed or yeast, full of promise of what is to come.

In terms of Jesus' parables, to pray for the coming of the kingdom is to pray for the growth of that mustard seed and for the rising of the dough until the shrub comes to full maturity and the dough becomes the bread of the Father's kingdom.

The second section of the journey narrative (13:22-19:48) develops important aspects of the petitions for our daily bread, reconciliation, and preservation from the test, and we shall examine these aspects in relation to those individual petitions in later chapters. For the present general contextual considerations, however, we should note Luke's return to the Samaritan theme and the emphasis on the Samaritan's gratitude upon being healed of leprosy (17:17-18). All the more reason why the disciples should not call down fire from heaven to destroy the Samaritans. Like the good Samaritan, the grateful Samaritan is a model to be imitated.

The story of the Samaritan's gratitude and Jesus' related teaching are followed by two parables on prayer. The first is on the need to persevere in prayer and not to lose heart when God does not seem to answer (18:1-8). Its themes are already familiar from the parable of the man who woke his neighbor to borrow some bread (11:5-8). The second is about a Pharisee and a tax collector at prayer (18:9-14). As in the

preceding parable, the point of the second parable is given in
the narrator's introduction (18:9): Some believed in their
own righteousness and, in their self-righteousness, held
everyone else in contempt. The parable shows how the tax
collector, who saw himself as a humble sinner and prayed accordingly, was justified and would be exalted. The Pharisee,
who exalted himself with head unbowed as he proudly
prayed, was not justified and would be humbled by God.

The Lord's Prayer is not a prayer for the self-
righteous. It is a prayer for those who recognize that they are
sinners and humbly ask the Father's forgiveness. Their prayer
is surely answered.

After the Lord's Prayer, and clearly related to it, the
most important prayer in the entire journey is in the journey's
last section (22:1-24:53), in the prayer event at Gethsemane
after the Last Supper. This passage, which includes Jesus'
prayer to the Father (22:42) is framed by the admonition that
the disciples pray that they might not be put to the test
(22:40, 46). Its relationship to the Lord's Prayer is unmistakable in both pre-Lukan tradition and Luke's gospel.
We shall study it in commenting on the final petition of the
Lord's Prayer. For the moment it suffices to recognize its
relationship to the cup of the Last Supper and to the blood of
that cup which falls on Gethsemane's ground as perspiration
while Jesus prays. Like the test of the Lord's Prayer, which is
related to our daily bread, the test of Gethsemane is related
to the cup of Jesus' self-offering as lifeblood shed for all.

Summary and Conclusion

The literary context of the Lord's Prayer in Luke 11:1-13 and
9:51-24:53 has sensitized us to the presence of the prayer's
themes in Jesus' teaching on prayer and in the Lukan journey
narrative. At times, the narrative provides an introduction to
the Lord's Prayer (11:1) and a commentary on praying it
(11:5-13). At other times, it develops its themes in larger contexts and spells out its implications for various facets of Christian life in history.

We observed how Luke emphasizes perseverance and

patience in prayer. We are assured that the Father answers the Lord's Prayer according to our needs with the gift of the Holy Spirit, and at the very moment we pray it. We have also seen that the Lord's Prayer must be prayed humbly and with charity for all.

We were able to describe the Lord's Prayer as the prayer for the Holy Spirit, the prayer of the Christian journey to the Father, the prayer of the Christian exodus, the prayer of the Christian mission, the prayer of those who see with the Son's own vision, the prayer of Christian neighbors open to all, and the prayer of Christians at prayer with Jesus at Gethsemane.

In the next chapter, we shall pursue our effort to penetrate the Lukan context by focusing on the prayer's relationship to the Christian community.

Two

The Lord's Prayer in the Christian Community

We have examined the Lukan literary context of the Lord's Prayer. While doing so we noted that the prayer was addressed to special people, Jesus' disciples, and in a very special context, that of Jesus' own prayer.

We now inquire into the identity of those special people. Who were the disciples and how did Luke see them? Indirectly, we shall also examine our own relationship to Jesus' addressees and open the way for a fruitful praying of the Lord's Prayer according to Luke.

The Lord's Prayer was intended for Jesus' disciples. Luke 11:1-2a makes this very plain. The request that Jesus teach his disciples to pray came from a disciple who spoke in the name of all the disciples. Jesus' response, which included the prayer and some further teaching, was directed not to that disciple alone but to all those he represented.

In the request Jesus' disciples are distinguished from those of John. Would Jesus teach his disciples to pray just as John had taught his disciples? John's prayer may have been adequate for those who responded to his prophetic call, but it did not express the unique identity of those who shared Jesus' vision and mission. Jesus' disciples needed a new prayer.

Luke's addressees in 11:2-4 consequently require our special attention. It is not that the disciples simply happened to be the prayer's first recipients and those who were to

33

transmit the prayer to others, irrespective of their own relationship to the Lord. From the prayer's brief narrative introduction (11:1-2a) there can be no doubt that the Lord's
Prayer should be approached, studied and prayed as a prayer
which was intended specifically for Jesus' disciples.

In this chapter we shall examine Luke's view of
discipleship. We shall also explore the way he presented one
of the most commonly recognized aspects of discipleship, the
following of Christ. Finally, we shall look at a special Lukan
aspect of discipleship and show how for him the disciples are
forerunners of the Lord's future coming as well as followers
of the Christ who already came.

The Prayer of Jesus' Disciples

To pray the Lord's Prayer in the spirit of Luke we must approach it as the prayer of Jesus' disciples. But even more important, we must see ourselves as disciples living in continuity
with those whose story fills the pages of Luke-Acts, and who
assume personal ownership of the Lord's Prayer. We might
otherwise understand the prayer intellectually, but it would
always remain someone else's prayer.

After a short examination of our modern context, we
shall explore the meaning of the term "disciple" in Luke and
discuss one of the major characteristics of discipleship, namely, the disciple's presence to Jesus the teacher.

The Modern Context

At one time, when Christians had much less religious
contact with those who were not Christians, the specifically
Christian nature of the Lord's Prayer could more easily be
taken for granted. Today, however, it must be emphasized.

At home and abroad Christians often find themselves
at prayer with men and women whose religious identity is
different from theirs. In such circumstances it is an easy
temptation to view the Lord's Prayer as a general prayer appropriate for all religious people, a prayer which cuts across
differences and gathers everyone into a fundamental religious

unity. People of good will, who respect the religious tradition and experience of others, all thirst for such a unity. Is God not the Father of us all? Surely God shows no partiality. All who fear him and do what is right are acceptable to him (Acts 10:34-35).

For the early Christians the view we have just expressed was unthinkable. It is true that God shows no partiality and that he welcomes everyone, as Peter indicates in Acts. But before joining Christians in praying the Lord's Prayer those invited had to accept the call to discipleship.

The issue is complicated by the contents of the Lord's Prayer, which never mention the name of Jesus and contain not one single christological title. Its address and petitions correspond to basic human aspirations. Could it not be a good Jewish prayer as well as a Christian prayer? At the level of language it certainly seems to provide the generic prayer we need. Many of its expressions are even reminiscent of prayers in ancient Judaism. Why should not all those who recognize God as Father join in praying it? By emphasizing the uniquely Christian character of the Lord's Prayer, are we not reinforcing tendencies toward religious exclusivism?

We certainly do not want to prevent others from joining us in praying the Lord's Prayer. However, our openness must not obscure the fact that those who pray it may be expressing quite different attitudes and needs. The words may be the same, but their content is bound to differ. For example, a Christian's notion of the kingdom is not the same as that of a Jew and even more different from the understanding which a Moslem, Hindu or Buddhist might have. For a Christian, the Father's kingdom is inextricably bound up with Jesus' proclamation of the good news and the role which his death and resurrection played in inaugurating it.

There is no dissociating the content of the prayer from the religious identity of those who pray it. How we view the "we," the "our" and the "us" of the second set of petitions is critical for understanding the prayer. In the Lukan context these pronouns clearly refer to men and women who see themselves as disciples, who hold certain values in common, and whose lives have come together in a shared experience.

Even as we pray with non-Christians, in recognition of a religious unity which transcends all differences, the prayer should remind us of our Christian uniqueness. As Christians we are called to make a special contribution to a religious world which is shared by many peoples of good will. This contribution is summarized in the Lord's Prayer.

The Disciples in Luke

What does it mean to be a disciple? An examination of the term's usage in the New Testament and more particularly in Luke-Acts is filled with surprises.

The term "disciple" *(mathētēs)* appears exclusively in the story of Jesus as told in the four gospels and in Acts, the story of the apostolic church. The term appears nowhere else in the New Testament. In its place Paul and others use expressions such as "brothers and sisters," "the elect" and the "saints." The term "disciple" is consequently associated with the Christian story, with early historical traditions of the life and mission of Jesus and the beginnings of the apostolic church, and with their retelling in narrative form. Other terms are associated with Christian preaching, with the prophetic tradition which dominates the letters and calls Christians to constant fidelity.

These observations provide an important clue to the meaning of discipleship. "Disciple" is a relative term and quite meaningless apart from a human correlative. In Mark, Matthew and John, that correlative is sometimes expressed by the popular Jewish term *rabbi.* There were many rabbis, of course, but for Christian disciples, *the* rabbi was Jesus. Writing for Gentile Christians, Luke avoided this Jewish term. Instead, his two volumes have the Greek word *didaskalos,* "teacher."

Jesus the teacher had his disciples, but so did others. Luke 11:2, for example, refers to the disciples of John. The same term was used when John sent his disciples to the Lord asking whether he was the one who was to come (Lk 7:18-23). In Luke 5:33 we have a reference to the disciples of John and of the Pharisees. Correlatively, John, whom Luke saw primarily as a prophet, was invoked as teacher by the tax collectors who had gathered around him in the region of the Jordan and who were attentive to his call for repentance and baptism (Lk 3:12).

As in the case of other disciples, those of Jesus were identified by their relationship to their teacher. The disciples of Jesus were those who gathered around him and whom he taught. Little by little their life was patterned on his teaching. The disciples were consequently a recognizable group which could be distinguished from other groups.

The word "disciple" is a general designation akin to the term "Christian." The relationship between the two terms is clear from Acts 11:26, where Luke says that the disciples were first called Christians at Antioch. Those who came to be called Christians had earlier been called disciples. Christians are disciples who recognize Jesus the teacher as the Christ.

In Luke the disciples are first mentioned in 5:30 at a banquet held by a tax collector in their teacher's honor. Their uniqueness is recognized by the Pharisees and their scribes who could not accept that Jesus' disciples could eat and drink with tax collectors and sinners.

Although the disciples are not named in Luke 5:30, we must assume that they included those who are mentioned in 5:1-11, Simon Peter, James and John. The impression given, however, as in all later references to the disciples, is that Luke had a larger group in mind, and that he expects readers to know about the disciples. The disciples are all those who later would be called Christians.

Those who become Jesus' disciples do not take this initiative on their own. To become disciples they have to be called by Jesus. Luke 5:1-11, which focuses on the call of Simon and presents James and John as his partners, helps us to understand the meaning of Jesus' call for all disciples.

Being a disciple is not the same as being acquainted with Jesus. At the time of his call Simon already knew Jesus and he even had assisted Jesus in fulfilling his mission. Simon was not yet a disciple when Jesus stepped into his boat and asked him to pull out a little from land in order better to address the people gathered on the lakeshore (5:1-3). Nor was

he a disciple when Jesus asked him to put out into the deep
(5:4). He showed himself open to discipleship, however,
when against all human odds he accepted Jesus' word to let
down the nets (5:5). After the extraordinary catch, which
opened his eyes to who Jesus really was, and in which he
recognized his sinful distance from the Lord and
acknowledged his sinfulness, he had all the necessary disposi-
tions. It is only at this point that Jesus called Simon to
discipleship and that Simon accepted the invitation together
with his companions. Henceforth they would go in quest not
of fish but of human beings (5:6-11). As in their fishing, they
would do so against heavy human odds.

Disciples are, therefore, men and women who may
have known Jesus humanly but who have also met him in
faith and acknowledged him as Lord. In so doing they
recognize that they are sinners with no right to the Lord's
presence. At the same time, however, this first response to
the Lord includes an implicit prayer for forgiveness, a prayer
which would become an important part of the Lord's Prayer.
When the Lord calls them and they accept, they enter into
his presence, forgiven and ready to join in his mission.

When Luke presents the Lord's Prayer as a disciples'
prayer, all of these conditions and qualities are presupposed.
To the extent that they are foreign to our experience, the
Lord's Prayer remains empty words. When the story of
Simon's call becomes our story, and we join him and his com-
panions as disciples, the Lord's Prayer becomes our prayer.

To appreciate our call to discipleship, we must pay
close attention to what we are called to. A great deal could be
said at this point, for Luke devotes many chapters to this
theme. One word, however, can summarize it all: presence.

In the Presence of Jesus

Simon's story in Luke 5:1-11 provides us with a model,
a paradigm, for understanding the disciples' presence to
Jesus.

First, the disciples are called into Jesus' presence. It is
then that he reveals himself as Lord. When they
acknowledge him as Lord, they become present to him. At

the same time, they recognize their sinfulness and cannot imagine that the Lord can remain present to them. They ask him to leave, but he does not. The Lord's presence is a reconciling presence. Later they may distance themselves from Jesus their Lord, like Simon after Jesus' arrest, but Jesus does not abandon them.

Presence in this context is obviously not a matter of physical proximity. In the early part of Luke 5:1-11 Jesus and Simon were together in the same boat, but they were not present to one another as they would be at the end of the passage. Presence is an awareness, a personal openness, an acceptance, an attentiveness, an active relationship. An act of presence invites a response. Without mutuality presence remains unfulfilled, just as when someone speaks but no one listens.

Presence is the basis of personal communication. Without it Jesus would not have been able to teach the disciples, and they would not have been able to learn from him. Consider the story of Martha and Mary. Mary was present to the Lord, and she listened to his word. Martha became too busy. Anxious about many things, she lost touch with the one thing necessary, the most fundamental component of discipleship, presence to the Lord and communication with him (Lk 10:38-41).

Presence is essential for every aspect of discipleship. It is also the most basic quality of the disciple at prayer. The disciples learned to be present in their relationship with Jesus. Through him they discovered the Father's presence (Lk 10:22). From him they learned to reciprocate with their own (Lk 11:2-4).

The Prayer of Christ's Followers

We have seen that the Lord's Prayer is a disciples' prayer, the prayer of those who are Jesus' disciples and who recognize him as Lord. We have also seen how being a disciple presupposes a call and a conversion experience in which the disciples are healed of their sinfulness and begin to live in the presence of Jesus.

We now examine how the disciples are followers of Christ, men and women engaged in a journey which is clearly mapped by the life of Christ. As with discipleship, we shall begin by looking at the modern context. We shall then explore the meaning of following Christ in Luke and discuss one of its major characteristics, namely, the follower's solidarity with Christ.

The Modern Context

For most of us the terms "disciple" and "follower" are so closely related that we often use them interchangeably. Not without reason. Both refer to the same people. Disciples are followers of Christ, or at least they ought to be. No one can be a true disciple without being a follower, and no one can be a follower without being a disciple. But this does not mean the terms are identical; each carries a slightly different nuance.

The word "disciple" is a designation for the circle of people who are taught by Jesus. It is a rather static term and calls to mind membership in a group or community. The word "follower," on the other hand, is anything but static. It refers to a way of living, one patterned on the way Jesus lived. The disciple is one who sits and listens to the teacher. The follower is one who walks in the teacher's footsteps and assumes his way of life and his mission.

Actually, being a follower is even more fundamental than being a disciple. In 5:1-11 Luke shows how Jesus' call to Simon and his partners was to follow him. Discipleship is only indirectly implied. We refer to disciples in reading the story because of later references and not because of the text of 5:1-11 itself. Those who have accepted the invitation to follow Christ subsequently become his disciples. The disciples are people who have previously accepted the call to follow Christ. At least that is the way it all began and how the New Testament envisioned things.

In our day the opposite is usually the case. Pastoral efforts focus on members of the church, including disciples in the most static sense, and try to bring them to the following of Christ. We try to inject new life and vigor into an old body. Jesus and the early Christians tried to teach and form a new body. In reading the New Testament we should keep this difference in mind. It can save us much frustration and help us to direct our efforts. It will also help us to appreciate what it means to pray the Lord's Prayer as the prayer of Christ's followers.

The Followers in Luke

What does it mean to be a follower? As with discipleship, the New Testament and Luke-Acts are full of surprises.

First of all, the noun "follower" never appears in the New Testament. Instead we always have the verb, "to follow." As already noted, the following of Christ is not a static notion. The New Testament's use of verbs to refer to it corresponds to the notion's dynamism. Disciples should not be passive (although they may be called "disciples" even if they are). However, followers, to use our language, are always active. If they become passive, they are no longer followers.

Second, "following" is a term associated only with Jesus, the Christ and our Lord, and with the gospel narratives which tell his story.[1] What is especially noteworthy is that the term's christological usage does not appear in Acts. In this story of the apostolic church, it was quite appropriate to refer to the disciples, an enduring body of people. Following, however, was so closely related to the person of Jesus that the early Christians may not even have thought of using it outside of his story. Through the teaching of the apostles the number of disciples grew enormously after the death-resurrection of Jesus, and Acts uses the term "disciple" quite frequently, beginning with 6:1-7. Acts even refers to the

1. The one exception is Revelation 14:4. This is a reference to those who followed the Lamb, a christological symbol, wherever he goes. The verb meaning "follow," a common enough Greek word, does appear in 1 Corinthians 10:4 and five additional times in Revelation, but in the ordinary sense of one thing coming after another in motion or in time. Even here, the very infrequent usage indicates that the term had acquired a very special meaning for Christians and that they hesitated to use it in any other sense.

disciples of Saul or Paul. Only Jesus, however, had followers. Paul's disciples were people whom he taught, but they were not people who followed him. Paul taught those who had accepted the invitation to follow Jesus the Christ.

Following Jesus means, first of all, leaving everything (Lk 5:11,28;18:28). By leaving everything, the gospel means turning away from a former way of living and from everything connected with it. At first reading this may appear rather negative, but only when leaving everything is seen as a prerequisite for following Jesus. Actually, it is an aspect inseparable from taking up the cross (Lk 9:23). Leaving everything and taking up the cross are two facets of the same reality, in which we undergo a change of values, attitudes and life orientations. By the very fact of taking up the cross, we leave everything.

The cross is a very important early Christian symbol. It stands for the passion and death of Jesus, of course, but also for the resurrection and glorification which he experienced through the cross. No other symbol summarizes the ultimate implications of all that Jesus did more succinctly and more forcefully. To follow Jesus is to walk with him through suffering to glory (Lk 24:26).

For Christians, taking up the cross is a normal consequence of the passion-resurrection with which Jesus' life climaxed. Luke introduces this most basic Christian challenge (9:23) immediately after Jesus' prophetic statement concerning his death and his raising on the third day. In this text, Jesus is presented as the Son of Man, a title which sees him as *the* human being, the one who best expresses what it means to be human and the human response to life which God intended for all human beings. In taking up the cross Christians show their solidarity with Jesus, the perfect human being. In doing so they are most true to themselves as unique persons. It is not Jesus' cross that they take up but their own.

The cross refers to every moment of life. Far from a remote challenge which we may someday have to face, it is ever present. Christians take up their cross "each day" (9:23), an expression which appears in the Lord's Prayer within the petition for bread. As we shall see, this petition, which refers to the breaking of bread or Eucharist, is closely related to Jesus' suffering, death and resurrection to glory.

Luke 9:57-62 develops the implications of taking up the cross and following Jesus each day. First, it requires a detached way of life, which finds no true home except in God. Second, it asks that we say good-bye to all that is dead—the dead are the concern of the dead, not of the living. The living proclaim the reign of God, that reign which is the object of the second petition in the Lord's Prayer. Third, it demands that followers not look back to what has been left behind. To do so is to abandon the following of Jesus. Only those who look forward are fit for the reign of God for which we pray.

Luke 18:15-43 emphasizes the social implications of the following of Jesus. To accept the kingdom is to leave all for the sake of the kingdom and to guarantee entry into the kingdom. Such acceptance requires that in leaving everything, we give to the poor. For Luke, sharing with the poor is one of the distinguishing marks of those who have embarked on the following of Jesus. In Acts 2:42-47 and 4:32-35 we see how sharing remained an ideal for the Christian community, even if it was an ideal Christians sometimes failed to reach (Acts 5:1-11).

The following of Christ, which is the heart and soul of discipleship, covers every aspect of Christian life. As with discipleship, however, it can be summarized in one word: solidarity.

In Solidarity With Christ

Solidarity actually springs from presence. It is the most basic quality of disciples who are followers. In calling his disciples Jesus invites them to join in solidarity of life and mission. In accepting his call they become one with him. His values become their values. His mission becomes theirs. They share in the good that he does, and they suffer with him in his rejection. As disciples, those called must learn all this. Their learning takes place in the presence of Jesus and in solidarity with his life as the Christ.

The disciples' solidarity is a response to Jesus' solidarity with them, a completely selfless solidarity which held back nothing, not even his own life, a solidarity which transcended even death and which would accompany them on their mission to the end of the earth.

The solidarity which following Jesus implied is perhaps best seen in the dialogue between Jesus and Simon Peter at the Last Supper. As in Luke 5:1-11, Peter recognizes Jesus as Lord. On this occasion, however, he does not ask Jesus to depart from him but proclaims his readiness to stay by his side even if this should entail imprisonment and death itself (Lk 22:33-34). Bold and self-assured words. A short time later, after Jesus' arrest, the gospel notes that Peter followed Jesus, but at a distance. In the courtyard of the high priest's house, this distance becomes a chasm as Peter repeatedly denies any association with Jesus. Rejecting all solidarity with Christ, he abandons the way of the follower, but only for a short time. Upon returning it is he who strengthens his brothers in their solidarity with Christ.

Christ's solidarity is not limited to his disciples. Every page of the gospel story witnesses to his solidarity with every human being. Christ's solidarity is a commitment unto death for the life of all peoples. The gospel also shows how those who follow him join in that same solidarity which he embodies. With Christ, the followers reach out in solidarity to the whole world. They become sacramental embodiments, effective signs and witnesses of Christ's commitment to bring the gospel to the end of the earth (Acts 1:8).

Following Christ in solidarity is no easy matter. In fact, when Jesus asked that those who followed him give to the poor, and when he pointed out how hard it is for the rich to enter the kingdom of God, those listening asked who could then be saved (Lk 18:22-26). Jesus' answer was that things that are impossible with men are possible for God (18:27). That is why we pray for the kingdom, for a self-sacrificing meal, for forgiveness when we fail and for perseverance and strength in life's ultimate test.

The Lord's Prayer is a disciples' prayer. It is also a prayer for those who have accepted the invitation to follow

Christ, who have left everything, who give to the poor, and who take up their cross each day in solidarity with Christ. Sharing Christ's mission and commitment, they are in solidarity with the Father, and so it is that they pray: ". . . hallowed be your name. Your kingdom come."

The Prayer of the Lord's Forerunners

The disciples were followers, as we have seen, but they were also something else. The disciples were forerunners. As followers the disciples saw their lives patterned on that of Christ and they walked in solidarity with him along a way which he pursued through suffering to glory. As forerunners they prepared the way for the Lord's return in glory.

We now take up the role of the disciples as forerunners. As in the two previous sections we shall begin by reflecting on our modern context. We shall then look at how Luke presents the disciples as forerunners and explore one of the salient characteristics of forerunners, openness to the Lord.

The Modern Context

One of the major features of modern times is change. As soon as we have adjusted to the new, it slips into the past. Every wave is followed by another, relentless as the sea. The change we experience is rapid, sometimes violent, and profound. Who can say what our world will look like in the year 2001? Those who dare to predict usually do so in symbolic terms, rarely in the realistic language of history, sociology, politics and economics.

In such circumstances, which affect the religious as well as the secular world, the church tends to respond like other international and national bodies. It feels an enormous need for mapping and planning its future course. It turns to the past which it can examine and where it knew how to respond. From the point of view of the present, the pace of change was much slower in the past, at least in the recent past. As with other institutions, it is only normal that the church should sometimes react negatively to the new, try to stem the pace of change, and opt for the old and tested. The

Vatican Council's statement that the church is in the modern world is more than an option. It is an inescapable fact, and it affects all of us for good and ill.

As we continue our efforts for renewal it is much easier to see ourselves as disciples, secure in the presence of Jesus, or as followers, pursuing a way of life which is already well-charted by Christ, rather than as forerunners, men and women who proceed into the future and prepare the way for the Lord's coming. It is precisely in this respect that our maps fail us.

The church must be open to the new and unforeseen, even as it patterns its life on the old in the following of Christ. The future has a way of prying open the past and showing how it can be lived in entirely new ways. We know what it meant to follow Christ yesterday. A renewed emphasis on the church's role as forerunner will help us to face the future as together we search for what it means to follow Christ today and tomorrow.

The Lord's Prayer has a clear future orientation. This is most obvious in the petition for the hallowing of the Father's name, the coming of his kingdom and our not being brought to the test. Given their context, the petitions for our bread and for forgiveness are also future oriented. We make these petitions for the present precisely because we want to contribute to the coming of the kingdom.

Emphasis on the forerunner aspect of discipleship and of the following of Christ helps us to pray the Lord's Prayer both according to Luke and according to the needs of our time.

The Forerunners in Luke

We saw that the term "disciple" appears only in the gospels and Acts and that the following aspect of discipleship is not found outside the gospels. The forerunner aspect is even more restricted. It appears exclusively in Luke. Unlike "disciples," however, for which we have a noun, and "following," which is found in various forms of the verb, we have no nouns or verbs to speak of the disciples as forerunners. Instead we have a prepositional phrase, "before him" *(pro prosopou autou),* which has an interesting history and whose use is very significant.

Both in and out of Luke a similar prepositional phrase, "before you" *(pro prosopou sou),* was used to express the role of John the Baptist, the forerunner who had prepared the way of the Lord (Mk 1:2; Mt 11:10; Lk 7:27). In every case the phrase is part of a longer quotation from Exodus 23:20, "Behold, I send an angel *before you,*" which was combined with a quotation from Malachi 3:1, "Behold, I send my messenger to prepare the way *before me*" *(pro prosopou mou).* The notion of forerunner and the special terms to express it thus entered New Testament tradition as a scriptural interpretation of the role of John the Baptist. In its combined form the text reads as follows: "Behold, I send my messenger before you." In the Old Testament the lines are attributed to the Lord God, who consequently refers to "before you," that is, before the people of Israel (Ex 23:20) or "before me," that is, before the Lord God himself (Mal 3:1). In its application to John the Baptist, "before you" is always used, but in this case *you* refers to Jesus the Lord. John the Baptist was the forerunner of the Lord's first coming.

When Luke applied the same expression to the role of the disciples, he modified it slightly to fit the narrative context. "Before you" became "before him" with *him* referring to Jesus the Lord (9:52; 10:1). In both passages the subject is now Jesus, rather than God, but the personal name Jesus is not used. Instead we find "Lord" (9:54; 10:1), a title which associated Jesus with the Lord God and which evoked Jesus' glorified state. As in Exodus 23:20, Malachi 3:1, and their application to John the Baptist, both 9:52 and 10:1 use the verb "send." "Messenger" (Mal 3:1), however, which remained singular for John the Baptist, is now plural, "messengers." John the Baptist was only one; the disciples are many.

From the above analysis, it is clear that Luke meant to compare the role of the disciples to that of John the Baptist. However, whereas John prepared the coming of Jesus in history, the disciples are sent to prepare the Lord's final coming in glory. That is why the prayer which John taught his disciples, a prayer which has long been lost, was not adequate for Jesus' disciples. They needed a prayer similar to John's, but one which reflected their own distinctive role in history (Lk 11:1).

The two passages in which the Lord Jesus sends his disciples as forerunners (9:52; 10:1) are found in the introductory section of the gospel's journey narrative, a journey which leads to the ascension and to heaven, where Jesus the Lord must remain until the time of universal restoration (Acts 3:21) which will take place at his return (Acts 1:11).

Luke's journey narrative must be read on three levels. There had been a historical journey to Jerusalem. In that journey the disciples related to Jesus the teacher precisely as disciples. It was consequently quite proper for Luke to refer to the disciples as disciples throughout the course of the journey.

The journey narrative, however, which was inspired by Mark 10:32-52, was written after Jesus' passion-resurrection. Like Mark, Luke thus presented the disciples as those who were following Jesus on that journey. The disciples' life journey was patterned on that of Jesus the Christ. To express this Luke used the verb "follow," but he also used a traditional prepositional phrase, "after me" (*opisō mou*, 14:27), a phrase which also appears outside of the journey narrative (9:23). On the journey the disciples came *after* Jesus the Christ (Mk 8:29), the Christ of God (Lk 9:20).

The theme which dominates Luke's introduction to the journey (9:51-10:37), however, is that of forerunner. The disciples not only came *after* Christ, they were sent *before* the Lord to prepare his coming. Since the forerunner theme is developed in the journey's introduction, the entire journey is first and foremost a long statement on the life of those who prepare the Lord's return in glory.

The Lord's Prayer, which Luke inserted in the great journey narrative (11:2-4), must consequently be seen as the prayer of disciples who followed or came after Christ but primarily as the prayer of forerunners, of those who went before him and whose mission was to prepare the Lord's definitive advent.

As forerunners the disciples need many qualities. The journey narrative develops these in relation to various contexts and shows how the forerunners live, act and think as they pursue their mission. Among all those qualities, there is one which summarizes them all: openness.

In Openness to the Lord

Like solidarity, openness is closely related to presence. It is hard to imagine how people could be mutually present to one another or to God without being open to the presence of others. But there is a big difference between openness and solidarity. Solidarity refers to a mutual presence which already exists and which springs from the history of Jesus the Christ with us. Openness refers to a presence which is yet to be, and it springs from a promise and the well-founded hope that it will be fulfilled in a presence which transcends every Christian dream.

Without such a hope all prayer would be nipped in the bud. We pray for something we do not yet have, but which we hope to have. The reasonableness of our Christian hope is based on God's promise and on our experience of how he has fulfilled his promises in the past. It is also based on our solidarity with a Christ who showed himself extremely open to God's will and saw God's promise fulfilled in the ascension.

Even so, hope is difficult to sustain, especially when we do not find it fulfilled when we think it should be or in the way we anticipated. Luke takes up these issues at several points in his gospel.

First he deals with the forerunners' impatience. When those whom the Lord sent before him were rejected in a Samaritan town, they asked if they should not call down fire from heaven to destroy those who had not welcomed them (9:52-55). Their intention evokes the action of Elijah in 2 Kings 1:10-12. Their mission, however, while it was comparable to God's messengers, John the Baptist and Elijah, would be fulfilled in a very different way. Patience and openness would have their reward, as we see in Luke

10:25-37 where Jesus shows how a Samaritan could be the true neighbor and a model for his disciples to imitate.

The theme of impatience recurs in Luke 17:22-37. As history unfolds, those who prepare the way of the Lord would find its tensions and problems difficult to bear. Jesus warns them of a time when they would long to see one day of the Son of Man (17:22). The day of the Son of Man, like the day of the Lord, refers to the final coming and the universal judgment. The disciples might not long for this day precisely, since it would involve them as well as all others, but might there not be just one such day, one of the days of the Son of Man, which would take care of their enemies? In this, they failed against openness. There was no avoiding suffering and rejection by the present age (17:25).

In their impatience the forerunners might lose heart. Responding, Jesus tells them a parable on the need to pray always. If a widow can finally gain her rights from a corrupt judge by persisting in her demands, surely God will grant justice to his chosen ones who persist day and night in calling on him (18:1-8). Recall the very similar parable told immediately after the Lord's Prayer: A man prevails on his friend to rise from bed and give him the bread he needs for an unexpected guest. So it is with those who pray the Lord's Prayer (11:5-9).

At times impatience is not the problem. The disciples pray, but they do not obtain what they requested. In 11:10-13, which also comments on the Lord's Prayer, Jesus continues to speak in parables. It may appear that the disciples have received a snake or a scorpion when they asked for a fish or an egg, but would any human parent among us, in spite of our sinfulness, respond this way to a child's request? Can we really believe that our heavenly Father would give anything less than the Holy Spirit to those who pray to him?

The Lord's forerunners thus need to pray with great openness. The fulfillment of their prayer for the hallowing of the name and the coming of the kingdom is in their Father's hands. They must resist the tendency to take matters into their own hands. Maintaining openness, they thus persevere in prayer, trusting that the prayer will be fulfilled. Their prayer is like that of Jesus at Gethsemane: "Not my will but yours be done" (Lk 22:42).

Summary and Conclusion

We have situated the Lord's Prayer in its Christian community context. In doing this we have reflected on our modern situation; shown how the prayer is the prayer of Jesus' disciples, of the followers of Christ and of the forerunners of the Lord; and developed a particular life quality which is critical for each of these aspects of Christian life in history, as Luke presented it.

Praying the Lord's Prayer as a prayer of Jesus' disciples, the major contemporary problem stems from our relationship to those who are not Christians. Even as we pray with them, we must be aware of the unique significance of the Lord's Prayer for Jesus' disciples. The disciples are those who have gathered in Jesus' presence to learn from him how to live, act and pray.

Praying the Lord's Prayer as followers of Christ, the major problem comes from our relationship to those who identify themselves as Christians and go through the motions of Christian living, but without seriously trying to pattern their lives on that of Christ. The Lord's Prayer means something quite different for those who take on the challenge of the kingdom as Christ did. The followers are those who join Christ in solidarity and remain with him to the end as he pursues his mission.

Praying the Lord's Prayer as forerunners, the major problem arises from our own tendency to block out the future in a time of rapid change which can appear extremely threatening. The Lord's Prayer addresses the new and unforeseen. It is not a prayer for those who constantly retreat into the past. The forerunners are those who go before the Lord in openness to him as they prepare his coming in glory.

The three qualities we emphasized—presence, solidarity and openness—are well exemplified by Mary's response to the angel at the annunciation: "I am the servant of the Lord. Let it be done to me as you say" (Lk 1:38). The Lord was present to Mary; she reciprocated by being present to him. God's plan of salvation was disclosed to Mary; she committed herself to that plan in solidarity. The fulfillment of God's plan was humanly impossible; she responded with openness, trusting in the power of the Holy Spirit.

As disciples, followers and forerunners, we join Mary and the apostolic community, devote ourselves to constant prayer (Acts 1:14), and await the Father's gift of the Holy Spirit (Acts 2:1-4; Lk 11:13).

Three

Luke presented the Lord's Prayer as the prayer of men and women who are disciples, followers and forerunners of Jesus. To pray the Lord's Prayer according to the scriptures, and more particularly according to Luke, we must see ourselves as disciples who are taught by Jesus, as followers who pursue the way he first traced, and as forerunners whose basic mission is to prepare his final coming. We studied this triple context in order to emphasize the unique identity of those for whom the prayer was intended. But how concretely did they, and do we, learn to pray the Lord's Prayer?

The purpose of this third chapter is to explore the experiential context in which Jesus taught the disciples how to pray. As in the previous chapter, its point of departure is Luke's own introduction to the prayer (11:1-2a).

The chapter includes three sections. First, we shall examine the disciples' experience of Jesus at prayer and show how the very need to pray is grounded in the disciples' association with Jesus while he prays. Second, we shall approach the prayer from the point of view of the disciple's request and see how it is truly the *Lord's* prayer and not just the prayer of Jesus. Third, we shall study the nature of the prayer from the point of view of a summary expression found in Luke 11:13 and show how fundamentally the Lord's Prayer is a prayer for the Holy Spirit.

53

Experiencing the Prayer of Jesus

In Luke's gospel Jesus teaches his disciples how to pray in the context of his own prayer. This context, which is uniquely Lukan, is quite different from that of Matthew.

In Matthew, the Lord's Prayer (6:9-13) is part of Jesus' teaching in the discourse on the mount, a synthesis of the disciples' attitudes and way of life. More specifically it forms part of a section on almsgiving, prayer and fasting. These practices illustrate a general principle of Christian living: Take care not to practice your piety before others in order to be noticed by them; otherwise you will receive no reward from your Father in heaven. Even more specifically the teaching is meant to counteract Gentile tendencies to multiply empty phrases as though the sheer volume of words could guarantee a divine hearing.

The disciples must avoid any outward display which could have lingered with them from their former association with the synagogue, and they must be careful not to be influenced by the Gentile environment in which they now pursue their mission. Jesus thus provides his disciples with a model prayer which will help them to avoid both of these dangers and guarantee that their prayer be authentically Christian.

The Matthean context of the Lord's Prayer shows how at a very early date the prayer was related to a special social context, that of the synagogue and its practice of prayer, and how it subsequently was applied to the world of the Gentile mission. It also helps us to see very clearly how the prayer formed part of the living gospel tradition, a tradition rich and versatile which was fully capable of meeting new challenges and circumstances.

Throughout this development the prayer's formal context was Jesus' teaching activity. Accordingly, Matthew focused on the prayer's wording, purity of intention, and simplicity.

The Lukan context is quite different. As in Matthew the prayer is taught, of course, but not as one of several practices. Nor is it taught in a formal teaching experience; its context is not that of Jesus teaching but of Jesus praying. The disciples' learning of the prayer and of how to pray it is directly linked to their experience of Jesus at prayer.

From Luke we learn not so much that the prayer must be prayed or that Christian prayer must avoid the pitfalls of the environment. We learn the dynamics and nature of prayer. Matthew was concerned with particular ethical questions surrounding the practice of prayer. Luke's concern was with the wellspring and art of prayer. To learn as did the disciples in Luke's gospel, therefore, we must examine the experience presented in Luke 11:1-2a and join those disciples in the same experience.

The narrative begins by presenting the setting: once while Jesus was praying in a certain place. At first reading the setting appears quite vague, especially when we recall Matthew's setting on the mountain. Luke refers to a place, but its location is completely undetermined. For Luke, who is frequently quite graphic in describing the physical setting for an event or teaching, this is unusual. The time or occasion for the teaching is also undetermined. All we know is that it was at some moment while Jesus and the disciples were on the journey to Jerusalem. We learn this not from 11:1 but from the introduction to the previous story and from the general context of this part of the gospel. Matthew at least indicated that it was when Jesus went up the mountain after seeing the crowds and when his disciples came to him. Luke simply presumed the presence of the disciples. He saw no need to introduce them explicitly.

In view of Luke's vagueness concerning the setting we might be tempted to move on. But in doing so we would never know what led one of the disciples to request that Jesus teach his disciples to pray. We can take it as a general principle that Luke's introductions, however brief, are significant.

To appreciate the Lukan setting we must be sensitive to the nature of time and place in cultures such as that of the New Testament. Their approach to these concepts may differ markedly from our own.

Western cultures tend to view time and place as objectively as possible. Time is given in minutes, hours and days, and it is measured by a watch or calendar. Place is given in feet or meters, and it is indicated by a map and geographical coordinates. This tendency is in keeping with the great value which we place on objectivity in our whole approach to reality.

The popular culture of the New Testament, however, saw little value in objectivity; the dominant value was subjectivity. Time and place were not seen or spoken of as objectively measurable. Instead, both were approached from human experience. Time was viewed as a sequence of events in which people proceeded from one thing to another, as when Jesus and his disciples went to the Mount of Olives after the Last Supper. In this context the conjunction of events and experiences is significant, not the precise moment which distinguished them.

Likewise the association of events and experiences is more important than their actual sequence. Otherwise Luke could hardly have presented all the resurrection events in chapter 24 as taking place on the same first day of the week. Judged by our objective standards, the day of the disciples' experience of the risen Lord was an impossible day.

Place is also indicated in relation to human experience; for example, Acts mentions that the Mount of Olives is about a Sabbath day's journey from Jerusalem (1:12).

When time and place are viewed through the prism of human experience, there is a tendency to speak of them in very concrete terms, and the two often blend into one. The meeting with Zacchaeus, for example, occurred when Jesus was passing through the city of Jericho (Lk 19:1).

The experiential element in indications of place and time may be so significant that it overwhelms every other consideration. It is as though place and time dissolve into the experience. Such is the case in Luke 11:1 when the narrator introduces Jesus at prayer. To the question, When did the disciple ask Jesus to teach his disciples to pray? we must answer, When Jesus was at prayer. Where did the disciple ask him? Where he was praying. The one thing which matters is that Jesus was praying. Everything else fades away. Jesus' prayer fills the entire time and place, both of which become one and disappear into Jesus' act of prayer. The disciples were there, completely taken up by the moment.

Such an experience is not a time for comments or for asking questions. It calls for silence and respect. As the narrative continues we are told that the disciple made his request only *after* Jesus had ceased praying.

With this analysis of the Lukan setting we are now in a good position to ask what moved the disciple to place his request.

First, the disciple had to recognize the enormous value of Jesus' prayer. He had to see Jesus' prayer relationship to his Father as something good and great in itself. Such appreciation is indicated by the fact that he made his request only after Jesus had finished praying. An interruption would have indicated lack of appreciation. Had the disciple broken into Jesus' prayer, it is quite unlikely that he would have done so with the request that Jesus teach his disciples to pray. We do not ask for what we do not appreciate.

Second, the disciple also had to recognize that he and his fellow disciples could not pray as Jesus had just been praying. There was something very special about Jesus' prayer, something so special that it led the disciple to sense a great distance between the way he and the others had been praying and the way Jesus was praying. They could pray like the disciples of John. Although Jesus himself had been John's disciple, however, his prayer was quite different from that taught by John.

Third, the disciple also had to recognize that the disciples, followers and forerunners of Jesus had to pray as Jesus prayed. Otherwise, how could they be fully his disciples, following in his way and pursuing his mission in preparation for his final coming? Their presence and solidarity with Jesus required that they pray as he prayed. His presence and solidarity with them, even as he prayed, sparked the disciple's request. Not to make the request would have been to abandon his following. In making it, the disciple was taking a further step in the following of Jesus and expressing his readiness to be a disciple in the full sense of the word.

To learn how to pray the Lord's Prayer according to Luke, we must be able to see ourselves in the disciple's position. We must have an experience of Jesus' prayer, and must share the presuppositions which led to the request that Jesus teach his disciples how to pray. Otherwise, we may learn all about the prayer of the early Christians as Luke presented it, but we will never learn how actually to pray as Jesus taught them to do. Knowing about the Lord's Prayer is not the same as praying it. Luke's intention is that his readers learn to pray. We must go beyond the message, which is but the tip of the iceberg, and open ourselves to the gospel's formative experience.

But where and when are we to come in contact with Jesus at prayer? Was not this a historical event tied to a special place and moment, an event in which only a few were privileged to participate? Did not Jesus' prayer and all possibility of experiencing it die with him on the cross?

Experiencing the Prayer of the Lord

Luke's own brief introduction to the Lord's Prayer shows how disciples who had not known the historical Jesus could experience his prayer. When the disciple turns to Jesus and asks that he teach his disciples how to pray, he does not address him as rabbi or teacher, as would have been the case during Jesus' teaching ministry. He addresses him as Lord, a title which was associated with the resurrection and which had become normal usage for post-Easter Christians who related to Jesus as Lord.

Luke thus took a title which properly belonged to Jesus' risen life and introduced it into his historical life. In a sense the practice is not unusual, and we ourselves follow it when we say, for example, "When Becky's mother was 5 years old . . ." or "When the bishop graduated from high school. . . ." Obviously the woman was not mother as a little girl of 5, and the bishop was far from ordination at his high school graduation. However, since the same person is now mother or bishop in relation to those to whom we are speaking, we do not hesitate to use these titles for a much earlier period.

So also with "Lord." In the context of Luke's gospel, which was written over 50 years after the resurrection, it was quite appropriate for the disciple to address Jesus as Lord. From the point of view of the story's setting in the life of Jesus, Jesus is addressed as one who would be Lord.

There is a major difference, however, between Jesus' title and that of other human beings. Titles like mother and bishop are read from one period of history into another period of history, from a set of historical relationships into a moment when those relationships did not yet exist. Lord, like Jesus' other post-Easter titles, is read from a life he now lives beyond history into a historical moment he once lived, from a set of relationships which join heaven and earth into a historical set of relationships. Seen from the point of view of the story's setting in the time of Luke and its prolongation into our own time and history, the title must consequently represent far more than a retroactive interpretation of history.

By introducing the title Lord into the disciple's dialogue with Jesus, Luke transforms the whole story into a communication event which breaks through the barriers of history and introduces historical disciples into the experience of the risen Lord. The story thus becomes that of Luke's readers, including ourselves, who identify with the disciple's request and make it their own. Like Luke's first readers, we too know Jesus as Lord and not as a teacher from Galilee on his way to Jerusalem.

Why then does Luke not speak directly of the Christian experience of the risen Lord, as Paul does in so many of his letters? Why does he present the story as though it pertained to Jesus' historical life? The reason is simple. Jesus is risen. We, however, continue to live in history. We have not yet joined Jesus in his risen state. Apart from history, life and even Jesus' prayer and teaching are incomprehensible to us. We need a Christian story about people in history. We need the story of the historical Jesus to give flesh to the experience we have of him as Lord. At the same time we need to hear Jesus speak as Lord, since that is how he now relates to us. The gospel story must leave no doubt that its principal actor has already moved beyond history and that we experience him as we experience no other. Hence the disciple addresses Jesus as Lord. As the disciple once spoke for all the disciples in Jesus' following, he now speaks for all of us.

The way Luke introduces the Lord's Prayer provides valuable insight into the prayer's early history. There can be little doubt that the prayer had its remotest origins in the prayer of the historical Jesus which, in turn, reflected the daily Jewish prayers of the time. However, it would be futile to try to attribute its fully developed form to the teaching of Jesus. Its two distinct forms in Matthew and Luke should alert us to this. In their present wording neither of these formulations corresponds literally to what Jesus taught, and neither can be used to measure the other as the one authentic prayer of the historical Jesus. Rather, the Lord's Prayer is rooted in Jesus' prayerful teaching, but its twofold development in Matthew and Luke springs from distinct formative experiences of the risen Lord.

For us, as for the early Christians, the Lord's Prayer is not just a prayer which Jesus once taught in the course of his historical life. It is a prayer which the risen Lord teaches to everyone who welcomes him in prayerful communion. But how can we recognize the risen Lord and experience him at prayer that we too may ask him to teach us how to pray? The historical context of the Lukan communities proves enlightening.

Like many of us, Luke's readers were aware far more of the absence of the historical Jesus than of the risen Lord's presence to them. It was hard to let go of the past and to accept that Jesus had died, no more to be present in history as he once had been. They clung to relics of Jesus' passing and kept looking to the tomb in which he had been buried. With this attitude, however, the tomb was meaningless, a symbol which reminded them only of what had been and of the death which occurred when their hopes were brightest.

Emptied of Jesus the tomb gave some indication that he was risen, but how could they really know without meeting the risen Lord? For many, life and hope had become as empty as the tomb.

The disciples had to learn how to leave the tomb, to accept that Jesus' historical life had indeed ended on the cross. This is the message of the two men who greeted the women when they came to the tomb on the morning of the first day of the week. Why do you seek the living one among the dead? (24:5). He is risen, among the living. Their message speaks across the centuries to all whose lived experience of the Lord has died, who no longer know where to find him or how to recognize him when they do. They may be looking in the wrong place.

The story of two discouraged disciples who abandoned the way and left Jerusalem for Emmaus shows how the living one can be recognized among the living (24:13-35). Today, as in Luke's time, the key which opens the eyes in recognition consists in generously sharing with those who would otherwise remain strangers to us. No one is a stranger at the Lord's table. Experiencing one another as brothers and sisters, we come to recognize the risen Lord, the Son whose life we share.

We know the risen Lord in the sharing of those who join us in the breaking of the bread, and others know him in us as we share with them. When the bread is broken in prayerful thanksgiving to the Father, we find ourselves in the presence of the Lord at prayer, recognize our own prayer's limitations, sense our need to pray as he does, and are moved to say: "Lord, teach us to pray."

The Prayer for the Holy Spirit

From our reflections on experiencing the risen Lord at prayer, it is very obvious that each of us bears the enormous responsibility of sacramentally revealing the Lord's presence to others, and that we must expect others to do the same for us. But how is this possible? After all, we are limited and sinful human beings who barely know how to pray. How can our act of prayer become an earthly incarnation of the ascended Lord's act of prayer?

Of itself it cannot. Only through the Holy Spirit, who breaks down our natural barriers and enables us to share without regard for race, ethnic origin, social class, nationality or sex, can we rise to the demands of Jesus' lordship. The Holy Spirit and the Holy Spirit alone transforms our gestures and sounds into the Son's prophetic deeds and words and elevates our yearnings and mutterings into a sacrament of the Lord's own prayer. Our prayer becomes the Son's prayer when we share in his sonship. Just as he was the Father's Son incarnate through the creative overshadowing of the Holy Spirit, we too become sons and daughters of the Father through the creative power of the Holy Spirit.

That is why Luke concludes the Lord's response to the disciple's request with a reassurance that the Father gives the Holy Spirit to those who ask him (11:13). The Spirit he gives is the Spirit of the Lord's Prayer, a Spirit which enables us to speak his prayer and allows all those with whom we pray to experience the Lord's Prayer as the disciples once did.

Luke-Acts is by far the richest of all the works in the New Testament in its teaching on the Holy Spirit. From the gospel's prologue to the end of Acts, Luke introduces the Spirit as the source of every major development in salvation history, as the creative principle of Jesus' historic life and prophetic mission, and as the energizing element which transforms ordinary men and women into disciples of Jesus who follow Christ and prepare the way of the Lord. Luke-Acts as a whole thus provides an excellent commentary on the Spirit's role in the life and prayer of Christians.

Of all Luke's passages on the Spirit the most basic are the annunciation of Jesus' conception and the visitation (1:26-38, 39-56). Taken together they provide an extraordinary summary of Luke-Acts' message concerning the Spirit's role in Christian life, history, experience and prayer.

Asked to give human life to the Father's Son, Mary wonders how this is possible since she does not know man. Gabriel answers that her conception of Jesus would not result from any human relationship or biological principle but from the Holy Spirit who would come upon her and overshadow her with the power of the Most High. With this, Mary accepts the call as the servant of the Lord.

Mary's vocation to bring the Father's Son into the world evokes and expresses the vocation of all Christians. Like Mary we are called to give historical life to the Son of God. As the human agent of Jesus' first advent in history Mary mirrors our sacramental role in Jesus' second advent as Lord. Troubled by the angel's word, wondering what his greeting meant and not knowing how of herself she could be mother to the Father's Son, she expresses our hesitations as we wonder how, with all our human limitations, we can possibly make the life of the risen Lord present in our world. With her we are told that there is no way we can do this on our own. The life we share becomes the Lord's life through the power of the Holy Spirit. The only condition is that like her we accept the invitation to be the Lord's servants.

After the annunciation Mary visits her kinswoman Elizabeth. Both Elizabeth and the child in her womb are filled with the Holy Spirit. Responding to Elizabeth's exclamations Mary speaks her *Magnificat*, a hymn of praise which echoes every theme in the Lord's Prayer.

In bringing the child conceived within her to her cousin, Mary reflects our own role in making the Lord present to one another. With Elizabeth we wonder that one who bears the Son's life should come to us. With both Mary and Elizabeth we exult at the Lord's presence. Quickened by the Spirit we look to the fulfillment of our Christian vision and mission, and the spark of prayer jumps to life in us.

Mary's *Magnificat* anticipates the fulfillment of the Christian vision. As a figure who represents the church and all Christians within it, Mary holds out that vision in promise. In the Lord's Prayer we engage ourselves in the mission which will transform that promise into a reality for all human beings.

In Chapters Five through Ten we shall develop these reflections on the dynamics of prayer and apply them to the address and the individual petitions of the Lord's Prayer. After studying the meaning of each phrase, we shall explore the experience of praying it with the Son and through the Holy Spirit.

Summary and Conclusion

We have now situated the Lord's Prayer in Christian experience. Like the first disciples our need to pray springs from an experience of the Lord at prayer. Recognizing the extraordinary quality of his prayer and that our own prayer falls far short of his, the experience moves us to ask that he teach us how to pray. Responding to our request the Lord teaches us to pray as disciples open to his presence, followers sharing solidarity of life with him, and forerunners open to his coming in future glory.

Our prayer is not just the prayer of Jesus, but the *Lord's* prayer, one which presupposes his passion, death and resurrection and which he teaches as the risen Lord. We come to know and recognize the risen Lord primarily in our breaking of bread, a sharing meal in which all become brothers and sisters, children of one Father, joined in the life of his Son, and in which no one remains a stranger. It is also there, in the breaking of bread, a prayerful act of thanksgiving, that we know the risen Lord at prayer and learn to pray as he does.

Our breaking of bread gives sacramental expression to the Lord's sharing and prayer, something it could never do without the Father's gift of the Holy Spirit. The Spirit introduces us to the Father's name and kingdom, moves us to share in the breaking of bread and to forgive everyone who is indebted to us, and strengthens us in life's definitive test. Through us the Spirit does the same for others, and our act of prayer becomes a new incarnation of the Lord's Prayer.

Like Mary we are called to open our lives to the Spirit and conceive and bring forth the Son's life. Like Mary's *Magnificat* our prayer is then sparked with the fire of the Holy Spirit. Resonating with the Lord's very own prayer, the prayer of the Father's beloved Son, it moves all who see and hear to ask, "Lord, teach us to pray."

Four

We have already seen how Luke's literary context for the Lord's Prayer is quite special; how it positions those who pray it as disciples, followers and forerunners; and how it grounds the Christian experience of prayer in the prayer of Jesus. In this chapter we shall focus on the text itself.

Our purpose is twofold. We want first to become aware of exactly what the prayer says. This requires special attention because we are so used to praying it according to Matthew, and even with the Matthean form, habit has dulled our perception and sensitivity to the words we pray. We must consequently open our eyes and ears to the prayer which the Lord teaches us as he long ago taught his disciples. Second, we want to grasp the prayer's structure as well as the function and interrelationship of its parts. Our purpose at this point is to acquire a deeper insight into a prayer we already see and hear.

We should thus discover, at least in a preliminary way, why the Lord's Prayer is the number one prayer for Christians of every age, time and culture.

Sharpening Our Vision

Our efforts to open our eyes and ears to see and hear what the prayer really says will proceed in two steps. We shall begin by looking closely at the text as we find it in the *Revised Standard Version*. Then, a look at the similarities and differences between the Lukan and the Matthean texts will increase our awareness of Luke's text still further, and we shall be well-prepared to examine the structure.[1]

The Revised Standard Version
        In the *Revised Standard Version* the Lukan text of the Lord's Prayer (11:2-4) reads as follows:

> Father, hallowed be thy name. Thy kingdom come. Give us each day our daily bread; and forgive us our sins, for we ourselves forgive every one who is indebted to us; and lead us not into temptation.

To become more sensitive to this wording, it is useful to write the prayer. This device, simple as it seems, guarantees a slow and attentive reading, and we are more apt to notice details.

        We are struck, first of all, by the prayer's brevity. Even without referring explicitly to Matthew we sense that various words and expressions which come spontaneously to our lips are missing. This experience is very similar to that of the ancient scribes. Rather than copy carefully from the text, they tended to do so from memory and to introduce elements which were familiar to them from Matthew and the liturgy.

        After copying the prayer with an eye fixed on the *Revised Standard Version*, it is good to read it again, this time from our own handwritten text. We thus read it as personalized by our own handwriting. Then we should try to rewrite what has already been written, but from memory. In doing this we are bound to recognize the temptation of the ancient scribes as our own, and we shall learn to overcome it.

1. Those interested in a deeper discussion of the text should refer at this point to the Appendix on page 165. The material in the Appendix provides for two additional steps in the study of the text of the Lord's Prayer:

    a) a comparison of the *Revised Standard Version* translation, a translation which is more literal than most, with that of *The New American Bible*, *The New English Bible*, and *The Jerusalem Bible*;

    b) a closer look at the wording of the Lord's Prayer, following the Greek text which underlies all of these translations.

Luke and Matthew

Next, a comparison of the Matthean and Lukan forms of the Lord's Prayer brings the uniqueness of the Lukan text into even sharper focus. We note two kinds of differences. First, Luke's form does not include a number of elements which are familiar to us from Matthew; it is much shorter. Second, when the two forms parallel one another there are important differences in wording. For clarity's sake we shall examine these two kinds of differences separately.

Form   Matthew's text (5:9-13) has many words and entire lines which are absent in Luke. The extent and importance of this difference are clear from the following parallel presentation. The Matthew column includes only the additional elements, not the differences in the elements which both have in common.

Luke *(RSV)*	Matthew *(RSV)*
Father,	
	our, who art in heaven,
hallowed be thy name. Thy kingdom come.	
	Thy will be done, On earth as it is in heaven.
Give us each day our daily bread; and forgive us our sins, for we ourselves forgive every one who is indebted to us; and lead us not into temptation.	
	But deliver us from evil.

We notice immediately that the Lukan text does not include Matthew's third petition, "Thy will be done." Nor does it mention "Our (Father) who art in heaven" or "On earth as it is in heaven." In Matthew's text these phrases tie the entire first part of the prayer, including the address "Father" into a single sub-unit. "Our," which in the Greek text follows the word "Father," corresponds to "on earth." "Who art in heaven" is paralleled by "on earth as it is in heaven." The absence of these elements in Luke help us to see how his one-word address, "Father," forms a sub-unit on its own, distinct from the petitions that follow.

We notice also that the Matthean prayer ends with a "but" clause which balances the previous negative petition with a positive one. Luke's form concludes with a negative petition. The significance of this will be explored in Chapter Ten.

Wording   Where Luke and Matthew have parallel elements some of the words are identical, but there are also many differences. Again the distinctive wording of each stands out when we place them in parallel columns. The Matthew column now includes only the variant formulations. Lines which are found in Matthew but have no parallel in Luke are omitted.

Luke (RSV)	Matthew (RSV)
Father,	
hallowed be thy name.	
Thy kingdom come.	
Give us each day	Give us this day
our daily bread;	
and forgive us	
our sins	our debts
for we ourselves forgive	as we also have forgiven
every one who is indebted to us;	our debtors;
and lead us not into temptation	

All the differences come in the petitions for bread and forgiveness. In Matthew the verb "give" is in the aorist, a form which expresses a single act. It asks that our Father give us our bread once. The verb form thus corresponds to Matthew's "this day." Luke's use of the present form calls for repeated giving and this corresponds to his "each day."

Notice also how Matthew refers to "debts" rather than "sins" and to "debtors," a Greek noun, rather than to being "indebted," which corresponds to a Greek participle. Nor does Matthew include Luke's "every one."

In Matthew, "as we also have forgiven" refers to something we have done in the past. In Luke, God's forgiving and our forgiving are simultaneous. Matthew compares what we ask our Father to do on our behalf with what we have already done on behalf of others. In Luke, there is no such comparison. The Greek text of Luke, however, does emphasize the fact that we ourselves *(autoi)* forgive.

The relationship between our act of forgiving and that of our Father is also indicated. In Matthew our forgiving is the basis, a prior condition which is the reason why our Father should forgive us. In Luke it is also the basis *(gar)* for the Father's forgiveness, but in quite another sense. Since the two acts of forgiving take place in the same moment, our forgiving of others is the act in which our Father forgives us.

Careful attention to these differences between Luke and Matthew indicates that our translation of Luke should avoid the kind of comparison which is found in Matthew. For this reason "ourselves" is better than "too." A good translation which links the two clauses ("and," *kai*) and shows how our forgiving is the basis *(gar)* of the Father's forgiving would be "*even as* we *ourselves* forgive." Note, however, that in this case, "as" does not establish a comparison. Rather it is temporal and indicates simultaneity. As we shall see these observations and conclusions are critical for understanding Luke's petition for forgiveness.

From the comparison of Matthew and Luke, along with a comparison of modern translations and a careful look at the Greek text (see Appendix), we thus arrive at the following translation:

Father
hallowed be your name.
Your kingdom come.
Give us each day our daily bread;

and forgive us our sins,
        even as we ourselves forgive
        everyone who is indebted to us;
and do not bring us to the test.

From Sight to Insight

It is not enough to be familiar with the form and wording of
the Lord's Prayer. We must grasp it as a structural whole
with parts which are functionally related to one another. We
have seen what the prayer says. We now want to have a
deeper insight into its inner workings. Such insight will help
us to understand the Lord's Prayer precisely as a prayer and
not merely as a collection of words and phrases.

We shall begin by considering the prayer's simplest
possible division, in two parts. Next, we shall refine this division, see how the prayer actually contains three parts, and
show the relationship among these.

Address and Petitions

In Luke the Lord's Prayer contains two sections: an
address ("Father") and five petitions. This division, broad as
it is, helps us to focus on the two fundamental ways in which
we speak to God in this prayer. First, we call on him,
"Father," much as we address someone by name before
speaking what we want to say or ask. Second, we develop
what we want to say, just as we do in ordinary conversation.
In this case, our statement unfolds in a series of requests.

As in human conversation, such a statement calls for a
response, especially since it is in the form of requests. The
way we began, addressing God as "Father," indicates that
we are ready and waiting for his response. Speaking to God,
however, is not like speaking to a human being. We wait in
silence, and God responds in our silence. Luke assures us of
our Father's affirmative answer. "Whoever asks, receives"
(11:10).

The five petitions in the Lukan text of the Lord's
Prayer sum up the entire gospel according to Luke. To ap-

preciate them we must see them as concise statements of the various themes which Luke develops at much greater length throughout his narrative.

Similar summaries can be found, for example, in the *Magnificat* (1:46-55), in Jesus' inaugural presentation in the Nazareth synagogue (4:16-30), in the composite Isaian quotation which Jesus reads on that occasion (4:18-19), and in the Last Supper account (22:14-38). In these instances the gospel is summarized in the form of a canticle or hymn of praise, a narrative, a prophetic proclamation, and a farewell discourse. In the Lord's Prayer, we find it in the form of a prayer.

Address, Vision and Mission

The two-part division provides insights into the general nature of the prayer and helps us to see how it relates us to God our Father. But grouping all the petitions into one unit makes it difficult to see how the prayer relates to the nature of Christian life. Everything in life is not of equal importance or on the same level. There are general purposes and goals as well as means to attain them. There are major relationships which focus life, and minor relationships which support them. So also with Christian life and with the prayer of Christians.

We gain a much deeper insight into the prayer by dividing the petitions into two parts. Such a division is required by the text's grammatical and literary form as well as by the content of the petitions.

> *Address:* Father,
> *Vision:* hallowed be your name.
>   Your kingdom come.
> *Mission:* Give us each day our daily bread;
>   and forgive us our sins,
>   even as we ourselves forgive
>   everyone who is indebted to us;
>   and do not bring us to the test.

The first part of the prayer has one element, a one-word address. The second part, here labelled "Vision," has two elements, brief petitions which in the Greek text are cast in exactly the same form. With extreme literalness, they look like this:

> hallowed be your name.
> Come your kingdom.

The third part, "Mission," has three elements, longer petitions with several qualifiers. These petitions are joined to one another by the conjunction "and," but vary considerably in sentence structure and grammatical forms. Unlike the first two petitions, those of the second set are not especially parallel to one another. Maintaining extreme literalness to the Greek, they are:

> Our bread, the daily (bread), give us
>   that (bread) each day;
> and forgive us our sins
>   even as we ourselves forgive
>   everyone who is indebted to us;
> and do not bring us to the test.

These observations are sufficient to divide the prayer into three parts, but they do not justify the titles we have given them. In the case of the address, there is no problem. Not so with "Vision" and "Mission."

Observing that the first set of petitions is characterized by the pronoun "your" and the second set by "us," "our" and "we," some call the first set the "you petitions" and the second set "we petitions." However, while these designations are grammatically well-founded, they do not take into consideration the content and the meaning of these petitions. Such designations could even be misleading. All too easily we might slip into thinking of the first set as though it dealt with God's concerns and of the second as though it dealt with ours.

There is no distinguishing the Father's concerns from ours. The name and the kingdom, of course, belong to the Father, and we acknowledge this in our prayer. But what reason would we have to pray for the hallowing of his name and coming of his kingdom unless these were our concerns as well as his? It is we, not the Father, who need the bread and the forgiveness and who do not want to be brought to the test, but why would we address these petitions to the Father unless we saw them as his concerns as well as ours?

In both instances the commentary on the petitions will support these preliminary observations. For the moment we need only add that the Father's name makes no sense unless it is disclosed to us and his kingdom is meaningless unless we are part of it. There is no question that we are profoundly involved in the hallowing of the name and the coming of the kingdom. Further, our bread, reconciliation, and fidelity to the end are all aimed at the coming of the kingdom and the disclosure of the Father's name.

A better way to distinguish the two sets of petitions, one which respects the unity of the prayer, is to see the first set in relation to the Christian vision and the second to the Christian mission.

The hallowing of the name and the coming of the kingdom begin in history, but neither is fully realized within history. Always on the horizon, even as we work for their fulfillment, they present an ideal which transcends every limited fulfillment and focuses all of our Christian life and efforts beyond history. Jesus himself proclaimed the coming of the kingdom. When he died, his disciples continued to do so. Now we do so, and when we die, others will continue to do the same. This is what we mean by "vision," something which stretches ahead of us, far beyond what can be realized in human history, let alone in our lifetime.

The second set of petitions deals with our social needs and commitments in history, every moment of history as well as in history's final climax. When the name and the kingdom are fully manifest, the gift of bread, the gesture of reconciliation, and preservation in the final moment will be no more. They belong entirely to Christian history and sum up every facet of the Christian mission. Unlike the vision, the mission can be realized in the present, and we can measure the quality of its fulfillment. The mission is what we are now involved in concretely as we look to the Christian vision. The vision keeps the mission on target and energizes it; the mission directs our energies realistically.

With regard to both the vision and the mission, we are altogether helpless. We know that of ourselves we can do nothing. That is why we pray, addressing God as Father, asking for the fulfillment of our vision and for all we need to carry out our mission, especially in the final test when all could be lost.

Summary and Conclusion

In this fourth and final chapter of Part I we looked at Luke's version of the Lord's Prayer as presented in the *RSV* translation; we compared the Matthean and Lukan versions of the Lord's Prayer; and we offered our own translation of the Lukan text. Our purpose was to become aware of the prayer's text as Luke handed it on to us.

The second part of the chapter examined the prayer's structure and the functional relationships among its parts. Dividing the prayer into two parts, we saw how the one who prays it relates to the Father, whom the prayer addresses. Further, dividing it so that it breaks into three parts, we saw how the prayer is related to the basic elements of Christian life: a transcendent vision which unfolds in the context of an earthly mission. With regard to both the vision and the mission, we are absolutely dependent on the gift of our Father, and that is why we pray.

Part II

Interpretation

Five

Father

The Lord's Prayer begins with a simple address, "Father"—one word, no more. The temptation to amplify and develop Luke's one-word address has always been strong. Should we not add at least the words of Matthew and say "Our Father in heaven" (Mt 6:9), as we find in so many ancient manuscripts of Luke, or perhaps "O Father, Lord of heaven and earth," as we read in Jesus' hymn of praise (Lk 10:21)? Yet Luke considered the simplest form of the address, "Father," to be sufficient.

Luke's one-word address was quite traditional, and it very likely came to him from the prayer's oldest form. The Matthean community, steeped in the ways of rabbinical interpretation, retained the word "Father," but expanded it by adding "our" and "in heaven," and thus drew the Christian prayer closer to that of ancient Judaism. The Lukan communities, whose social context was Gentile, were not influenced by these Jewish sensitivities.

Our effort to appreciate the Lukan form of the address will proceed in two steps. First, we shall focus on the meaning of the word "Father" as it applies to God and explore its implications for the self-understanding of those who pray it. Second, we shall examine the act of praying to God as Father and the kind of communication it entails.

Meaning and Implications

Luke's prayer opens with the Greek word *pater*, "father."
His gospel will help us to grasp what he understood by that
word, but first we shall examine its use in other early Christian writings. Like us, Luke did not live and write in a
vacuum.

Abba, Pater, Father

Among all the New Testament contexts where God is
referred to as Father, Mark 14:36, Romans 8:15 and Galatians 4:6 are especially pertinent for understanding the address of the Lord's Prayer. In each of these texts the Greek
word for "Father" is included as the translation for the
Semitic expression, *Abba*. In Mark, *Abba* is the address
which Jesus used in his prayer at Gethsemane. In Paul's letters to the Romans and Galatians *Abba* is a one-word prayer
which Christians used to address God.

Both Jesus and the earliest Christians used *Abba* in
their prayer to God. But with the passing of years and Christianity's expansion into the Greek-speaking world, it became
necessary to translate the word. The early Christians
recognized that their prayer had to spring from their own
culture. For Greeks only a Greek word would resonate with
the many experiences associated with the term "father."
Hence the *Abba, ho pater* of Mark, Romans and Galatians.
That the Greek Christians continued so long to say *Abba*,
even when it had to be translated, witnesses to the depth and
resilience of the Jewish tradition which was the point of
departure for all further developments, even outside of the
Jewish Christian context.

Eventually the translation *pater* replaced *Abba*
altogether in early Christian prayer, and it is this translated
form which was used in the Lord's Prayer in its Matthean as
well as in its Lukan form. *Abba* was dropped even in the
synoptic parallels of Mark's Gethsemane account (Mt 26:39;
Lk 22:42). In Greek the address continued to express the
warmth, love and respect which had once characterized the

Abba of Jesus and the earliest Christians. Our English address, "Father," does the same.

Simple as the address appears, *"Abba," "patẽr"* and "father" can mean many things. As applied to God, the address acknowledges that God is the source of life, like a human father who is a source of life for his children. We draw an analogy with human parenthood and the parent-child relationship. But what is the nature of that relationship? And what life are we talking about when God is its source?

Father-Child

Let us begin by exploring the father-child relationship. Our tendency is to approach this relationship from the fact that we have a human father and, in relation to our human father, we are children. Consequently, our calling God Father is ordinarily based on the experience which we have of our human father.

In both Matthew and Luke, the address "Father" is surely based on a parent-child analogy. However, it may come as a surprise to find that in both gospels the human image for father comes not so much from our experience of having a father as of being one.

In Luke 11:11-13 we do not read "Which son among you expects his father to give him a snake if he asks for a fish . . ." or "If you children receive good things from your earthly father. . . ." Rather we read, "What father among you . . ." and "If you, with all your sins, know how to give your children good things, how much more will the heavenly Father give the Holy Spirit to those who ask him." The image of God as Father clearly springs from our active experience of being father and giving life rather than from the passive experience of having a father and receiving life. Matthew has similar sayings in the sermon on the mount (7:9-11), but not in the section which deals with the Lord's Prayer (6:5-15). In Luke, however, the sayings are included among the verses which comment on the Lord's Prayer and continue the Lord's teaching on how disciples should pray (11:5-13).

For the Lord's Prayer the analogy's active point of reference makes an enormous difference. When we say "*Abba*," "*Pater*" or "Father" we relate to God as adults, not as little children. We relate to him as adults who know what it means to be father, who know the feelings of parents toward their children, and who appreciate the expectations which their children can, may and should have in their regard. Consequently, when we say "Father" we do so with the warmth, intimacy, love and respect which adults have for their father, and not with the attitudes of a little child who does not know the joy and responsibility of being a parent.

Father, Son and Spirit

In addressing God as Father, we have a human analog, but God's way of being Father is like no other. Luke presents the uniqueness of God's fatherhood first in relation to the life of Jesus, the Savior, Messiah and Lord (2:11). By insisting on Mary's virginity in the annunciation account Luke dissociated the mode of Jesus' conception from all other conceptions. Jesus' life can be understood only in terms of his divine origin. God is his Father, and he is the Son of God. Born of the Holy Spirit his origins transcend all considerations of human sexuality and every human relationship and principle (1:26-38).

At Jesus' baptism by John the Baptist we learn that his life and mission also transcend earlier expressions of God's fatherly relationship to Israel. Jesus' religious mission does not flow from John's baptism. The Holy Spirit descends on Jesus not during the baptism or while he was emerging from its waters but after the baptism while he is at prayer. As in the annunciation scene, his being God's beloved Son springs from God's creative Spirit (3:21-22).

Rejoicing in that same Holy Spirit, Jesus praises his Father when the seventy-two disciples return from their successful mission (10:1-22). He praises him for what he revealed to the disciples and those who welcomed them. This revelation was first given to the Son, and it is through the Son that all others come to know the Father. That is, it is through the

Son that they come to know the Father precisely as Father by sharing in the life which he had given his Son.

From Jesus' hymn of praise, we learn that God is our Father in a very special way. He is our Father because we share in the life which Jesus received through the power of the Holy Spirit. At Pentecost the source and nature of our divine life was revealed in the descent of the Holy Spirit on the apostolic community (Acts 2:1-4). All of Acts is the story of how that life is to be deployed in history.

Pentecost, an act of divine fatherhood, could come only after Jesus' resurrection. The life of Christians in the Spirit is a share in the risen life of Jesus our Lord. The life which God gives us is consequently far more than the human life which he gives us as creator.

The life of those who know the risen Lord and live by his life is also quite different from that of the disciples during Jesus' earthly life. Like Jesus, they may have turned to God and addressed him as Father. After Jesus' passion-resurrection and the event of Pentecost, however, their life was transformed, and God was Father for them in a brand-new way.

When we pray to God as Father, we do so as men and women who have been gifted by the Holy Spirit, who share in Christ's divine sonship and in the life of the risen Lord. We pray *"Abba, Pater,* Father" as adult men and women who know how to give good things to our children.

Dynamics

Knowing the meaning of the word "Father" does not make it a prayer. As with all the other elements of the Lord's Prayer, understanding the language is but a first step. We may know the lexicon, the grammar and the syntax, but we never really know the language until we actually speak it to someone.

Recall that the disciples did not ask the Lord to explain a prayer to his disciples or to lay out the meaning of its words, but to teach them how to pray. To grasp Jesus' response we must explore the Christian dynamism of speaking the word

"Father" to God. Only then will we come to appreciate
Luke's message as a gospel-transforming word. For Luke the
Christian address to God as Father was not merely a source
for reflection on the theological meaning of God's
fatherhood. Like Jesus, his purpose was to teach us how to
pray.

Praying to God as Father
The difference between understanding the meaning of
the word "father" and praying to God as Father easily can be
grasped from viewing the ways adults relate to their human
father.

First, it is possible for adults to know that a particular
man is their father and to know many things about him. In
this, they know facts. For the facts to be significant, they
must know what it means to be a father as well as what it
means for a particular individual to be their father. In this,
they grasp meaning.

Second, adults can go beyond facts and meaning and
accept someone as their father. In doing so their knowledge is
no longer merely objective. They know someone from within
a personal relationship. Medieval philosophers and
theologians referred to this kind of knowledge as a knowledge
of connaturality. When adults accept someone as their
father, they know him personally and relate to him and address him as their personal father.

Third, adults can respond to the invitation and actually address someone as father. In doing so, they know him in
an entirely new way. Addressing someone as father is like a
verbal embrace, an opening to his self-communication and
fatherly care. The relationship is personally transforming.

From this human analog we see that there are many
ways of viewing the Lukan address of the Lord's Prayer. We
can approach it as a message. God is our Father, and Luke
tells us many things about him. On the basis of Luke's faith
we accept the fact and recognize something of its meaning.
We can also approach it as an invitation to accept God as our
Father and to relate to him personally. When we do so our
knowledge of the Father moves from the objective to the sub-

jective plane, and it expresses our own faith as well as Luke's. This experience, however, is but a beginning, a promise which needs to be fulfilled in transforming knowledge.

In Luke 11:2 Jesus not only tells the disciples that God is their Father, he asks them to pray to him as Father. Luke's own intention in presenting the episode is the same. When we hear his message, accept his invitation and actually pray "Father," Luke's purpose is attained and we reach the summit of Christian faith experience.

With the Son

Christians hear the invitation to accept God as Father in their association with the Son. They accept the invitation and actually pray "*Abba, Pater,* Father" with the Son, Jesus, the Christ and our Lord.

Our prayer to God as Father is consequently not a one-on-one experience. It presupposes the incarnation, that God's life has been revealed in the person of Jesus, that he offered us that life by laying down his human life, and that he continues to reveal it in his presence as Lord. When we address God as Father, we do so as men and women who know the Son personally and share his life.

It is not incidental that the disciples were taught to pray "Father" by the Lord (Lk 11:1). What they prayed was the Lord's Prayer, one which they learned from the risen Lord's relationship to the Christian community, and not just the prayer of Jesus, which they might have learned in their past experience of the historical Jesus. They prayed the Lord's prayer with the living Son. Every time they said "Father," the Son taught them what it meant for God to be their Father. Jesus and the Lord may have taught the disciples, followers and forerunners how to pray in the past, but his teaching continues throughout our history. In the company of the risen Lord, we never cease learning to pray "Father."

Nor is it incidental that the disciples learned to pray while the Lord himself was at prayer. When they prayed "Father," they joined the Son in his *Abba* embrace, and their personal experience of the Father went from transformation to transformation. When Jesus the Son is the norm, a whole lifetime is not enough to know God as Father.

But how do we know the Son today, so many centuries after the death of Jesus? He lives in the community, apostolic commitment and prayer of the church to which we belong. He lives in our very imperfect and limited prayer. How then can we hope to know the Father and pray to him as we ought? Only through the Spirit.

Through the Holy Spirit

The Holy Spirit, the personal creative power of God through whom the Son was conceived (Lk 1:35), by whom he was driven into the desert for testing (4:1), and whose presence constituted his anointing as the Messiah or Christ (4:18), was also the vital source of Jesus' prayer to the Father (10:21). Through our association with the Son that same Spirit is the source of our prayer.

In Luke's time this realization was already solidly inscribed in Christian tradition and awareness. When Paul referred to our crying *"Abba"* to the Father (Rom 8:14-16; Gal 4:6-7), he attributed the cry to the Holy Spirit, the Spirit of God's Son which attests to our being God's children by adoption. The Spirit is also the reason why the *Abba* of our fellow Christians and our own *Abba* is not only the Lord's prayer but the Lord's praying. Christians thus learn to pray the Lord's Prayer in the experience of the Lord's praying in their community.

The Spirit, however, is more than the source and energy of prayer. It is its object. Jesus, whose entire being was penetrated by the Spirit from his conception and who rejoiced in the Spirit when he prayed, was also continuously open to receiving the Spirit. The Holy Spirit was the source of Jesus' growth and development as well as his origin. We see this in his post-baptismal prayer which was answered by a visible descent of the Spirit (3:21-22). When we pray *"Abba"* or "Father," the Lord expects us to be equally open to the Spirit. In fact, the Father's gift of the Spirit sums up all the petitions of the Lord's Prayer.

When we address God as Father, we accept him as the source of our life in and through the Spirit. We also ask to grow in that life. In effect we ask to be more and more open to his self-revelation or name and to his dominion or kingdom. We ask for the bread which joins all people at the Lord's table, for personal reconciliation in our mission of reconciliation, and for steadfastness in praying "Father" when we are finally tried like Jesus was tried at Gethsemane.

The Spirit thus provides the divine life-energy which allows others to experience the Lord's praying in us as we go before him to prepare his way.

Conclusion and Prayer

Luke's simple one-word address, "Father," sums up the entire Lord's Prayer. When we turn trustingly to God and address him as Father with the Son and through the Holy Spirit, we grow in personal knowledge of him and are increasingly transformed into sons and daughters worthy of his name and kingdom. When we pray "Father," the Lord continues to pray in us, inviting all who experience our prayer to ask, "Lord, teach us how to pray like you taught others how to pray." Answering through us, he says, "When you pray, say 'Father.'"

> *Abba*, the prayer of Jesus;
> *Abba, Pater*, the prayer of the early Christians;
> *Abba, Pater*, Father, the prayer of today's Christians.

> We come to you, Father, as grown-up children,
>   gifted with life,
>   and giving life to others.
> We know you, Father, through your Son,
>   whose risen life we share,
>   and whose Spirit we welcome.

> *Abba, Pater*, Father,
>   fill our lives with love and trust
>   as you filled that of your Son;

fill us with your Spirit,
that others may know your Son at prayer
and join your family in praying
Abba, *Pater*, Father.

Six

Father,
hallowed be your name

After addressing God as Father, the Lord's Prayer continues with a series of petitions. In both Luke and Matthew the first of these calls for the hallowing of the Father's name. Sober and unadorned, the Greek form of the petition opens with a verb, "hallowed be"; continues with the subject, "the name"; and adds a pronoun, "your," a direct reference to the Father. A bold request in the imperative, a humble plea in the passive.

The petition, "hallowed be your name," comes as the first of two which look to the Christian vision and at the head of the entire series which addresses the Christian mission. For both Luke and Matthew this first petition, which stems from the prayer's earliest form, provides the foundation for all the petitions which follow it. Fully adequate and more than satisfactory, it required no additional development or change of wording from the prayer's remotest origins to its inclusion in the gospel narratives.

In our analysis of this first petition, we shall again proceed in two steps. First, we shall explore the significance of names, the background and meaning of the Father's name, and what it means for the Father's name to be hallowed. Second, we shall examine the dynamics of the prayer that the Father's name be hallowed.

Meaning and Implications

Luke's own gospel and Acts show us what he meant by a name, the Father's name, and the hallowing of the name. Other early Christian works also prove helpful, since Luke's work reflected an emerging religious culture which already had seen a half-century of diffusion and development.

Names

It would be hard to exaggerate the significance of names in the ancient world. Even a superficial acquaintance with antiquity shows the importance of having a name, giving a name, changing a name, calling someone by name, and recognizing a name's meaning. Perhaps we were struck by this phenomenon for the first time while reading the Old and New Testaments, but it was altogether pervasive, both in and out of the Semitic milieu.

We often find, for example, that the original names on ancient monuments have been chipped away and replaced by others. We also come upon statues in Egypt in which a pharaoh has his feet firmly planted on the inscribed names of conquered peoples.

In the scriptures we read with attention how someone's name is changed. Abram becomes Abraham; Jacob becomes Israel; and Simon becomes Peter.

In Luke-Acts the author frequently goes out of his way to mention a name even when the original readers, let alone future readers, could not be expected to have known the person named. At times a name is spoken with great sensitivity and respect, as when Luke says, "the virgin's name was Mary" (1:27). Some names are so important that they are divinely ordained. Zechariah is to name Elizabeth's son John (1:13). Mary is asked to name her son Jesus (1:31). What accounts for all this attention to names?

The answer is not far to seek. For the ancients, as for many cultures today, a name was so intimately associated with the person who bore it that it was actually identified with that person. To be without a name was to be nobody. To step on someone's name was to tread on the person.

The name also expressed a person's role and human relationships. Accordingly a change of name meant a new place in life and history, a new posture with regard to others, new responsibilities, and a new way of relating.

The name also represented a person's personal disclosure and self-communication. Names are words. Like all other words, their purpose is to communicate. But only the name, a person's most intimate word, evokes that person's uniqueness and reveals it to others. Hence Luke's attention to names and the care with which he presents them. When someone's name is said to be directly from God or a divine messenger, we should understand that the person's role in history is divine and that the name given is rich with divine revelation.

The Father's Name

Small wonder that the Lord's Prayer is concerned with the Father's name. Could anything else introduce us more directly and more profoundly into the world of divine revelation?

The Father's name is the Father's person revealed. All of the scriptures and our own faith experience witness to God's revealing word, a revelation whose words accompany every moment and aspect of human life and every possibility and level of communication. Among these words, the Father's name stands above every other as the word which utters his own personal presence.

But what is the Father's name? Neither Luke nor any other biblical author tells us. In Exodus 3:14 God reveals his name to Moses and says that he is "I Am." We are taught the name of God, the name of the Lord, the God of our fathers, the God of Abraham, the God of Isaac, the God of Jacob (Ex 3:15). We are not given *the Father's* name. Since names express a person's identity, not in itself but in relation to others, would we not need a special name for God in his relationship to us as Father?

But is it possible for anyone to know the Father's name? To know it, would we not have to enter into the very source and divine mystery of life itself? Would we not have to enjoy the fullness of life and be sons and daughters equal to the Father? Only Jesus, the Son, no one else, received the Father's life to the full. For us it is more than enough to meet the Father in the Person of Jesus the Son, through whom we participate in the Father's life.

We do know, of course, that the Father has a name, and that word alone, "name," a common noun, enables us to meet him and to open ourselves to his revealing presence. In this, we are supported by the name's revelation to Moses as the one who is; that is, the one who is with us, nourishing, guiding and protecting us through life's exodus journey. We are also enriched by its revelation in Jesus as a transforming and saving presence for disciples who follow Christ and prepare his return as Lord. In the Son we know the Father's name in the limited manner suited to our human and historical condition (Lk 10:22).

Since Jesus the Son is the only one who really knows the Father's name, we can understand why every gospel reference to the Father's name is attributed to Jesus. Since knowing the Father's name could only take place in intimate communion with him, we can also understand why references to his name are found almost exclusively in contexts of prayer and worship.[1]

These observations concerning the gospel context for the Father's name suggest that Luke's petition concerning the hallowing of his name sprang from a fertile tradition of Christian prayer, which found a natural home in the early baptismal (Mt 28:19) and eucharistic liturgies (Jn 17:6,11,12,26). This association between the name and prayer had roots in the Jewish prayers of the time, but its life and spirit came from the prayer experience in which Jesus the Lord knew and revealed the Father's name.

---

1. The two exceptions are John 5:43 and 10:25, but even these occur in discourses given on the occasion of a Jewish feast (5:1) and on the feast of the Dedication (10:22). Apart from Matthew 28:19, which draws on a baptismal formula current in the Matthean community, every other reference is in a prayer which Jesus addressed to his Father (Jn 12:28, 17:6,11,12,26) or taught his disciples (Mt 6:9; Lk 11:2).

Hallowing the Father's Name

To hallow is to make holy and to be hallowed is to be made holy. It all seems so clear. But what does it mean to hallow or to be hallowed, and who is responsible for hallowing the Father's name? The ultimate responsibility must rest with the Father himself, since the petition is addressed to him. Were this something we could accomplish on our own, we would have no reason to include it in our prayer. But then, why is the petition not actively expressed to read, "Father, hallow your name"? Somehow we ourselves must have something to do with the Father's name being hallowed.

By approaching the petition from a Lukan standpoint—and through related passages in John—we see very well why the petition is passively expressed. Only the Father can bring about the hallowing of his name, but he cannot accomplish this without his children. Responsibility for hallowing the Father's name rests with the Father as the giver of life and with his children as men and women who receive and share that life.

In Luke, this is clearly expressed in the *Magnificat.* Mary sings her praise in terms which are very close to those of the Lord's Prayer: "Holy is his name." Yet Mary's song is also very different from "hallowed be your name." We look to the future and pray that our Father's name be hallowed; she reflects on the past and proclaims that God's name already is holy.

Mary's proclamation rests on her experience of the Lord's greatness and of his being her savior. God's name is holy because he has accomplished great things for her and fulfilled his promises made to our fathers, to Abraham and his descendants forever, establishing his kingdom, nourishing the hungry, extending mercy and upholding his servant to the end (1:46-55). The *Magnificat's* relationship to the Lord's Prayer and its concerns for the holiness of the Father's name, the coming of his kingdom, and his gifts of bread, merciful reconciliation and strength at the definitive fulfillment of life and history is clear.

Mary, however, proclaims that God's name *is* holy,

that the vision already is realized. As one who received the Son at his first advent, Mary anticipates and symbolically expresses the church's fulfillment of her mission at the Son's second and definitive advent, when the church too will be able to proclaim that the Father's name is hallowed. For Mary, God's name was hallowed because she had accepted the call to be his servant by welcoming the Father's Son in openness to the Holy Spirit. So will it be with us at the Son's return, and it is for this that we now pray saying: "Father, hallowed be your name."

John's gospel also provides an excellent window into the spirit and tradition which underlies this petition. Early in his gospel we read that Jesus comes in the Father's name, that is, as a manifestation of the Father's person (Jn 5:43). In God's personal Word made flesh, we have seen the glory of an only Son who comes from the Father full of love and truth (Jn 1:14). Even at the Father's side, the only Son continues to reveal him (Jn 1:18). In his very person, Jesus is the revelation of the Father's personal word or name, and all of his works are performed in his Father's name (Jn 10:25).

This brilliant Johannine theology, apart from the explicit mention of the name, can also be found in Luke 10:22 which speaks of the relationship between the Father and the Son and of the Son as the one who reveals the Father. Indeed the language and message of Luke 10:22 are so Johannine that many scholars refer to the verse as a Johannine intrusion. Intrusion may not be the best word, but it does highlight the fact that here and in many other passages Luke and John have numerous themes, attitudes and faith perceptions in common.

Another illustrative passage is the discourse in John 12:23-28, which corresponds to Luke's narrative of Jesus' prayer at the Mount of Olives (Lk 22:39-46) as well as to the Lord's Prayer. John has no Gethsemane narrative of his own. Instead we have this brief discourse which follows the anointing at Bethany and entry into Jerusalem and precedes the Last Supper.

Jesus' discourse is on the approaching hour for the Son

of Man to be glorified. It deals with the significance of that hour, how the laying down of one's life is the beginning of eternal life, with the hour's implications for Jesus' followers and with Jesus' own accepting attitude toward it. Jesus' soul is troubled, but he does not ask his Father to save him from this hour. In Luke, on the other hand, we read, "Father, if it be your will, take this cup away from me; but let not my will but yours be done" (Lk 22:42). The difference between the two gospels stems from John's emphasis on the Son's absolute oneness with the Father. Even in John, however, the question of preservation from the hour arose, but only as a rhetorical question which others might pose and which Jesus sets aside, and not in the form of Jesus' prayer.

The last statement in the discourse in John's gospel is a prayer, "Father, glorify your name" (Jn 12:28), which is clearly related to Luke's "Father, hallowed be your name." Accepting the hour and his glorification, Jesus prays that his Father's name be glorified. For John, the glorification of the Father's name takes place through the glorification of the Son of Man in whom the Father's personal word or name was made flesh (Jn 1:14).

The relationship between the hallowing and the glorifying of the Father's name and the petition's implications for the life of Jesus' followers becomes plain from the prayer which concludes Jesus' farewell discourse at the Last Supper (Jn 17:1-26).

Jesus had made his Father's name or person known to those whom the Father had given him (Jn 17:6; see Lk 10:22). Jesus had received the Father's name or personal presence and guarded his disciples with it. He now prays that his *Father* most *holy* protect those disciples with the name which had been given to him. The Father's name is his personal revelation as holy, most holy, and in its holiness, it protects the disciples at the hour of Jesus' exaltation to glory.

Jesus' glory is the gift of the Father's love, a love which Jesus shares with all believers. With that Father's love, he gives all who believe the glory which the Father gave to him.

At the end of the prayer, John once again returns to

Jesus' revelation of his Father's name. Even in glory, he will continue to reveal that name, so that the Father's love for him may always live in those who come to believe.

For John, the Father's name thus reveals his holiness, and like the Father, it is holy. It expresses the all-holy Father's protective love and grants a share in the Son's own glory to all who receive it in faith. The Johannine prayer, "Father, glorify your name," is consequently an alternative development of the early Christian petition, "Father, hallowed be your name." In line with John's emphasis on glory, it asks for glory, the effect, the fruit of the love which flows from the Father's name. Although Luke was not insensitive to Jesus' entry into glory, he retained the petition's most ancient form and prayed for the holiness of the Father's name, a holiness which overflows in love and glory.

Dynamics

We have examined the background and meaning of the first petition. We looked at its words, saw what it evoked, and analyzed its meaning as a Lukan statement. We now can explain what it means for the Father's name to be hallowed.

But what does it mean when we actually pray it and say, "Father, hallowed be your name"? As with the invocation *"Abba, Pater,* Father," it is one thing to understand the statement as the word of Jesus the Lord and the word of Luke, as the word of God spoken to us for our instruction; it is quite another to do what the Lord asks, to enter into the dynamics of the prayer we have been taught and to actually pray. By praying "hallowed be your name" we rise to an entirely new plane of experiential understanding.

Hallowed Be Your Name

The difference between understanding the petition as God's word to us and praying it as our word to the Father is best grasped from a comparison with the way adults address one another by name in ordinary conversation.

First, it is possible to know someone's name. However, unless we know the person who bears the name, it is meaningless. On the other hand, when we do know the person, the name evokes the person and conjures up all the experiences associated with that person.

Second, it is possible to have been given a person's name by the person whom it reveals and to have accepted that name. The name's acceptance takes place in the reciprocal gift of our own name. When names are mutually shared, those who have given and received them are united in a very personal relationship and have a special claim on one another's attention. To withhold one's name or to reject another's is to refuse this claim.

Third, those who enjoy a relationship of shared names can express that relationship by calling to one another by name, as when God calls to Abraham (Gn 22:1,11) and Samuel (1 Sm 3:10), and when the Lord Jesus calls Martha (Lk 10:41) and Simon (Lk 22:31) to loving attention and watchfulness. When the name is called, the personal relationship becomes electric. Those whose names are united in mutual knowledge know one another, not just in general, but in a new and unique moment which reflects all that has happened since the name was last spoken and which invites further knowledge in the immediate future.

I once heard someone call out to Hubert Humphrey as he was preparing to board a plane during the last months of his fatal illness. "Hubert!" Senator Humphrey turned and responded, "Jim!" In that moment, friends were united in warmth, appreciation, anticipation and full awareness that there would not be many other such moments.

In the same way, when we call on the Father's name, the current flows and our relationship to him becomes electric. We know him in a unique moment which is defined by our present situation and the way we are responding to it. In doing so, however, we express more than warmth and respect. We open ourselves to the Father's personal presence and, by this very fact, his love extends to us and his name is hallowed in a new moment of receptivity. As we repeatedly do this, we grow in faith and advance closer to the full manifestation of the vision of glory when all will be able to say with Mary, "Holy is his name."

With the Son, Through the Holy Spirit

We are not alone in hallowing the Father's name. We do so with the Son to whom his name was fully disclosed and in whom it is revealed. We do so through the Holy Spirit, which makes us sons and daughters with the Son. That is why Acts refers to the preaching of the gospel, Christian witness, the performing of apostolic wonders, and baptism as being in the name of Jesus Christ (2:38;3:6,16;4:10;8:12), in the name of the Lord's holy servant (4:30) and in the name of the Lord Jesus (8:16). To call on the name of the Lord is to reform and be baptized in the name Jesus Christ (2:38). There is no salvation in anyone else and no other name in which we are saved (4:12).

All of Christian life, from the hearing of the gospel to salvation, and all apostolic activity, conducted in the name of Jesus Christ, are lived and exercised through the Holy Spirit. The apostolic community received the Spirit on Pentecost. We receive it whenever we open ourselves to God's creative presence. Our collaboration in the hallowing of the Father's name, as in all the other petitions of the Lord's Prayer, springs from the Father's gift of the Spirit.

When in the Spirit we call on the name of Jesus Christ, the Lord's holy servant and the Lord, he becomes present to us and reveals himself anew. With his name, the name of the Father's Son, we then call on the Father's name, and the Father's name is hallowed in a manner which far surpasses our personal limitations. The Son reveals the Father to us (Lk 10:22), and with the Son we contribute to the hallowing of the Father's name whenever we pray, "Father, hallowed be your name" (Lk 11:2).

Conclusion and Prayer

Like the address, "Father," the first petition is the basis for all the other petitions and it includes them all. The hallowing of the Father's name expresses and actualizes our relationship to the Father from the point of view of revelation. In speaking that prayer we look in hope to the name's full disclosure and contribute to the Christian vision's unfolding in history.

Thanks to the Son in whose name we pray and the Spirit who empowers us to pray, the hallowing of the Father's name, like the kingdom, is already in our midst even as we look forward to a further and final revelation which transcends our present openness and possibilities.

> *Abba, Pater*, Father, hallowed be your name.
>> The prayer of Jesus;
>> the prayer of the early Christians;
>> the prayer of today's Christians.

> With love and respect, Father, we call on your
>> name,
>> revealed in your Son,
>> in whose name we pray.
> In holiness, Father, we bear your name,
>> sons and daughters fired with the Holy Spirit,
>> a Spirit of prayer and holiness.

> *Abba, Pater*, Father, hallowed be your name.
>> May we give it Mary's welcome,
>> ponder it in our hearts,
>> and speak it to the whole world,
>> that all may join your Son
>> and those to whom he revealed it in praying
>> *Abba, Pater*, Father, hallowed be your name.

Seven

Father,
hallowed be your name.
Your kingdom come

The second petition, "Your kingdom come," is just as short and simple as the first. In fact its Greek wording closely parallels the first. It begins with the verb "come," continues with the subject "the kingdom," and concludes with a pronoun "your," which relates the kingdom to the address, "Father." In each of these details, Matthew and Luke stand in perfect agreement. We can safely affirm that the second petition comes to us unchanged from the prayer's earliest expression in Christian tradition.

In Luke the petition, "Your kingdom come," concludes the set which focuses on the Christian vision. After praying for the Father's self-communication in revelation and faith, we pray for his manifestation in the transformation of persons and society. The vision thus includes the two basic components of the Father's presence to creation and history: his presence in word (name) and his presence in deed (kingdom). The same two components summarized the work of Jesus, a prophet powerful in deeds and word (Lk 24:19).

Like the Lord's mighty deeds and words, the Father's name and kingdom are closely related. In a theological analysis they may appear as components, but in a synthesis they are but two facets of one reality. The Lord's deeds are meaningful, and his words are effective. His wonders are significant, and his signs are wondrous. In the same way the

Father's name is transforming, and his kingdom is revelatory. The name and the kingdom, their hallowing and their coming, are thus two aspects of a dynamic reality in which signs (word, name) are effective (deeds, kingdom). We describe this reality as sacramental.

In our analysis of the second petition, we shall proceed as we did with the first. After explaining the significance of kingdoms, the background and meaning of the Father's kingdom, and what it means for his kingdom to come, we shall examine the dynamics of praying that the Father's kingdom come.

Meaning and Implications

Kingdoms are political realities. To understand what Luke meant by the kingdom of the Father, we must first explore, at least briefly, the political context in which Luke spoke of the Father's non-political kingdom. We must also examine the kingdom's relationship to Jesus, who came into conflict with earthly kingdoms as he worked for the coming of the Father's. Finally, we must see why we should pray for its coming when, as Luke says, the kingdom is already in our midst.

Kingdoms

Jesus and the early Christians lived in a world of kings and kingdoms, where power was absolute and its exercise discretionary. There was the empire, created by the genius of Augustus and marked by his successors, good and bad. Closer to home there was the Herodian family and the Roman prefects and procurators. There were also the Nabatean kings across the Jordan, the memory of Alexander, and a heritage of Ptolemaic and Seleucid rulers in nearby Egypt and Syria.

At every level, near and far, there were kings, and kingdoms were a fact of daily existence. For Jesus and others who made their way in the long wake of the vanished kingdom of David, living in a kingdom could be taken for granted. There had always been kings who reigned, and their rule had an enormous influence on religious institutions such as the Temple and the priesthood.

Like no other evangelist, Luke took pains to insert Jesus' gospel story into the context of earthly kingdoms. From the beginning of the prologue, "in the days of Herod," to the decree of Caesar Augustus and the Syrian census, and to the reign of Tiberius Caesar and the days of Pontius Pilate, the governor, Herod, Philip and Lysanias, the tetrarchs, and Annas and Caiaphas, the high priests, he carefully situates religious history with regard to the Roman empire.

In the ancient world it was not the structures but the impact of empires and kingdoms which impressed both citizens and noncitizens. Nor was the office as such of those who were kings and governors impressive, but rather the personal appropriation of that office, the way it was exercised in ruling and the glory of those who held it, a glory translated into pomp, display, public acclaim and adulation.

For Luke and others the word "kingdom" *(basileia)* thus designated two things. First, it referred to organizational structures, territorial limits, and a kind of government, as it does today. Second, it referred to a set of personal relationships among rulers and the ruled. For this second sense, active and relational words like "rule" and "reign" are better than the static word "kingdom." That is why English translations of the New Testament fluctuate in using "kingdom," "rule," and "reign" for the same Greek word *basileia.*

The political context of New Testament times and the way kingship was personally exercised were bound to influence the life of the early church. Then, as now, the church lived in the modern world and expressed itself within its structures. Accordingly the Lukan communities had to be exhorted not to act like the kings of the Gentiles who lord over their subjects and are called benefactors (Lk 22:24-25). In the kingdom of God those who are good leaders and truly great are those who serve the others (Lk 22:26-27).

The Father's Kingdom
Like Mark and John, Luke frequently referred to

"kingdom of God" or "reign of God." The corresponding Matthean expression was "kingdom of heaven." In substituting the word "heaven" for "God," the Matthean community followed the well-established Jewish· practice of respecting God's name by not speaking it.

Matthew's Jewish sensitivity influenced even the wording and meaning of the Lord's Prayer. After "your kingdom come," Matthew's gospel has a third petition, "your will be done," and adds the expression "on earth as in heaven," which qualifies the entire first set of three petitions. The theme of this expression had been introduced in the address, "Our Father in heaven." In the Matthean interpretation of the prayer, the name, the kingdom, and the will are actually hallowed, established, and done in heaven where our Father dwells. In the Lord's Prayer, we pray that what is true of heaven be realized on earth as well. The kingdom in Matthew's petition is consequently that of the heavenly Father, a nuance which is consistent with his gospel's many references to the kingdom of heaven.

Luke was not insensitive to the Father's being in heaven (10:21;11:13), but the Jewish milieu which influenced Matthew and the Matthean tradition of the Lord's Prayer did not affect its Lukan formulation and interpretation. For Luke the kingdom was the Father's kingdom, not that of our Father *in heaven.*

In our interpretation of the petition we must consequently be careful not to be influenced by the popular Matthean expression "the kingdom of heaven" which so easily comes to mind whenever we think of the kingdom. In Luke we do not pray for the earthly coming of a kingdom which already is established in heaven. Rather, we pray for the fulfillment of a kingdom which already is in our midst, but in promise (Lk 17:20-21).

Neither must we reduce the notion of kingdom to "the kingdom of God," an expression which we know so well from Mark's summary of Jesus' proclamation ministry (Mk 1:14-15) and introduction to the parables (4:26-32). This second tendency is particularly strong since Luke himself frequently referred to "the kingdom of God." In the Lord's

Prayer God is addressed as Father, and just as the name is the Father's name, the kingdom is the Father's kingdom, one which effectively reveals the Father's life.

Our clearest understanding of the Father's kingdom comes from the story of the Son, a story which shows him proclaiming the kingdom and working for its coming. In Luke and his fellow synoptics, no other expression is so intimately associated with the gospel and its proclamation.

The Father's kingdom is first introduced in the gospel's prologue in Gabriel's message to Mary at the annunciation. As the Son of the Most High, Jesus' divine Father, Jesus will be given the throne of David, his human father. But his reign over the house of Jacob, unlike that of David, will be without end. As David's son, Jesus will rule as king in David's kingdom, but in a manner far transcending that of his royal ancestor. In Jesus' reign David's kingdom becomes a perfect incarnation of the Father's rule over all human beings.

The *Magnificat* shows how the Father's kingdom confronts all earthly kingdoms and effects an extraordinary reversal of values. As Mary sings, the mighty are deposed from their thrones and lowly subjects are raised to high places (Lk 1:52). The Son's rule is nothing short of revolutionary, but like the kingdom itself, the revolution which brings it about is like no other. Joseph and Mary abide by Caesar's decree in going to Bethlehem for the birth of the savior king, the Messiah and Lord. However, David's city proves unable to grant hospitality to David's heir, thus assuring his transcendent rule as the first-born of a new people (Lk 1:6-7). Already we are alerted to the nature of the Father's rule, which would come through the Son's dying to lesser royal claims and aspirations.

The Coming of the Father's Kingdom

Luke's entire gospel can be read as the story of the coming of the Father's kingdom. From the beginning of Jesus' ministry at Nazareth (4:16-30), Jesus, the Son by the power of the Spirit which is ever upon him, comes into conflict with the blindness of the synagogue. His purpose, however, is not to condemn the blind but to give them recovery of sight. He wants them to see that the Father's reign has to embrace all peoples and that they must join with him in realizing it. To no avail. Irony of ironies, the effort to crush the Father's universal rule would contribute to its coming.

The Nazareth episode, which introduces Jesus' ministry, also summarizes its story, beginning with Jesus' first proclamation in the synagogue and the reaction of those who heard him. The effort to throw him over the cliff corresponds to the passion, where the Son would be victorious over human kingdoms. His passing through the midst of the angry mob and going away evokes the resurrection and the ascension, when Jesus would enter into the kingdom. This little gospel in miniature, and the story of kingdoms in conflict which it introduces, had been well-prepared by the account of Jesus' temptations in Luke 4:1-13.

The story of Jesus' encounter with the devil reveals the transcendent nature of the conflicts involved in bringing about the kingdom. Luke wants us to understand these conflicts in more than merely human and historical terms. At bottom, the struggle to establish the Father's dominion over earthly kingdoms pitted the Spirit of the Most High, Jesus' Father, against the spirit of evil.

The devil's price for earthly dominion over all the world's kingdoms was simple. God's Son had only to prostrate himself in homage before the devil. To fulfill the devil's vision of a world of many kingdoms which would be ruled by one man, Jesus would have to abandon his call to inaugurate the Father's rule of peace and justice over all peoples. Compromise was out of the question, as Jesus saw so clearly when he defended himself against accusers and said that every kingdom divided against itself comes to destruction (Lk 11:17). The kingdom of Satan could not possibly serve the kingdom of the Father.

Through the Son, the Father's kingdom was given to Jesus' disciples, little flock that they were. Accordingly, they were to place no store in the treasures of earthly life. They must seek their Father's kingdom over themselves and all else would follow in turn (Lk 12:31-34).

Like the Son, those who shared in his sonship and inherited the kingdom and its dominion would come into constant conflict with Satan. At every turn, however, they would be upheld by the Lord's own prayer, a prayer which he made for them that, like Peter, they might strengthen their brothers and sisters (Lk 22:29-32).

Nowhere is the conflict between the Father's kingdom and the rule of evil so dramatic as in Jesus' interrogation by Pilate and Herod (Lk 23:1-25) and in the crucifixion (Lk 23:32-43). The accusations brought against Jesus were that he called himself the Messiah and king, that he subverted the nation by opposing the payment of taxes to Caesar, and that he stirred up the whole people in Galilee, Judea and even Jerusalem, with his teaching. When Pilate asked him whether he was indeed the king of the Jews, Jesus answered neither yes nor no. "King" was Pilate's term. How could he have answered? His position on paying taxes was already well-known: "Give to Caesar what belongs to him, and to God what is his" (Lk 20:25).

Jesus was being accused of seeking his own kingdom, yet his whole life had been a vibrant rejection of earthly kingship, as we saw in his response to the devil's second temptation (Lk 4:5-8). Jesus worked for the coming of the Father's kingdom, not his own. In that kingdom the Father had granted him dominion and he had passed on that dominion to those who stood loyally by him in his temptations. His dominion had nothing to do with the way of earthly kings. Those who shared in it rejected this world's power, authority and recognition. Their life was rather one of service, and that is how with Jesus they would contribute each day to the coming of the Father's kingdom (Lk 22:24-30).

Jesus' accusers, however, did everything they could to force him into the position of an earthly ruler and the public stance he had rejected. In mockery, Herod and his guards even placed a magnificent robe on him. For them the robe expressed what they insisted was Jesus' royal pretense. For the readers of Luke's gospel it is the robe of the Father's kingdom. The irony of the royal robe would be surpassed only by the inscription which was placed over Jesus' head as he hung on the cross: "This is the king of the Jews" (Lk 23:38). By giving his life on the cross in the ultimate act of service, Jesus revealed the coming of the Father's kingdom. Commending his spirit into his Father's hands, he entered his reign. Receiving the throne of his father David, he inaugurated a rule which would be without end.

Dynamics

We have examined the notion of kingdom and how it influenced the life of Jesus and his disciples. We looked at the kingdom or rule of the Father, and how it differed from that of earthly kings. Finally, we explored Jesus' royal mission for the coming of the Father's kingdom, how it was consummated by his death on the cross and entry into his Father's reign, and how he passed the dominion he received to those who stood loyally by him in his temptations.

We now take up the dynamics of praying "your kingdom come," remembering that we have already opened ourselves to a hallowing communion in the Father's name. It is one thing to understand the prayer and its implications, but what does it mean to pray it? When Christians pray for the coming of the Father's kingdom, it actually comes, progressively, until the day of its full establishment when prayer will be no more.

Your Kingdom Come

Prayer is an act, not just words. Those who pray for the coming of the Father's kingdom open their minds and hearts to the Father's dominion. The very act of praying brings about what the words "your kingdom come" pray for. In praying, we receive, find and enter the Father's kingdom even as we ask, seek and knock (Lk 11:9-10).

In Jesus' life and prayer, the kingdom was already in our midst. The disciples sensed this when he prayed in their presence, and one of them asked that he teach them how to pray as he did. When they and we pray the prayer which the Lord taught his disciples, the presence of the kingdom intensifies and spreads, and it becomes more and more true that the Father's kingdom is in our midst.

Every time we sincerely pray for the coming of the kingdom, therefore, we do so from a new starting point. We build on the presence of the kingdom which was realized when last we prayed. The reign of God is indeed like a mustard seed which has been planted and yeast which has been mixed into the dough (Lk 13:18-21). As we pray that mustard plant grows and the bread continues to rise.

Each moment of prayer actualizes the Christian vision of the Father's kingdom a little more and adds to the feeling of urgency which spurs us to pray for the kingdom. The more we experience the kingdom's presence, the more we appreciate its blessings and the more we suffer from its absence. Praying propels us forward in prayer as we reach for the full realization of the Christian vision.

As disciples, this is the way we learned to pray. As followers, we learned to do so in a life journey whose full course has already been traced by Christ. As forerunners, prayer engages us more and more intensely in preparing the way for the Father's kingdom over us at the Lord's definitive advent.

Prayer is not an isolated act, independent of everything else we do. To be genuine it must express what we are all about. In Jesus' prayer this was clearly the case. When he prayed for the kingdom, he was asking his Father to bring about the vision which dominated his whole life and mission. It is the same with us. The prayer, "Your kingdom come," sums up our Christian commitment and plunges us further into the mission. Accordingly, the quality of our prayer can be measured by the degree to which we actually live and work for the coming of the kingdom.

Like Christ we can expect our commitment to the kingdom to threaten anyone whose reign is out of step with the Father's, and to evoke a negative reaction. At times, as we see from the experience of dedicated Christians around the globe, it even brings on persecution. In pursuit of the Father's kingdom, where human beings are free, where dominion is exercised in the form of service, and where local or national interests are subordinate to the good of all humanity, many lay down their lives as Christ had to do. Those who pray for the kingdom put everything aside, take up their cross and follow Christ into the Father's reign.

With the Son, Through the Holy Spirit

We do not pray alone. Our prayer is with the Son and through the Holy Spirit. How else could we fix our sights on so high a vision? The disciples first learned to pray for the kingdom in the company of Jesus at prayer (Lk 11:1), in the company of one whose life, mission and prayer were born of the Holy Spirit (Lk 1:35;3:21-22). Like Jesus, we too are baptized in the Holy Spirit (Lk 3:16).

Apart from our relationship to the risen Son and the Father's gift of the Spirit, we could hardly be expected to transcend our selfishness, our penchant to dominate, our need for aggrandizement and acclaim. The gospel and Acts show how strong these tendencies are and how difficult it is to break through the religious and political boundaries we keep erecting around us. Possessiveness governs our attitudes toward those who fall within those boundaries. Exclusivism prevents us from reaching out to those outside. With the Son and through the Spirit, however, we can break through and work for the coming of the Father's kingdom over all human beings.

Prayer and work for the Father's kingdom covers every aspect of life, but there are events in which all our efforts are gathered into one, moments when we celebrate our part in the kingdom which already is in our midst and when we proclaim its future coming. Those events are summed up in the petitions for the Christian mission, the second set of petitions in the Lord's Prayer.

The prayer for our daily bread and for reconciliation, both of which focus on the Christian meal, and the prayer for preservation from the test, which asks that we be able to follow through on the meal's implications to the end, are intimately related to the coming of the kingdom. Like the act of prayer the reconciling meal actualizes our vision here and now and moves us toward its fulfillment. The Christian meal, which we call Eucharist, marks the sacramental presence of the kingdom's coming in human life and society. Sacramentally the vision is now as we go about our mission journey to the Father: "Happy is the one who eats bread in the kingdom of God" (Lk 14:15). Happy is the one who prays with the Son and through the Holy Spirit for the coming of that kingdom.

Conclusion and Prayer

The first petition, "hallowed be your name," looked to the Father's self-communication in human life and history. The second, "your kingdom come," addresses his transforming presence over persons and society. Together these two complementary petitions sum up our Christian vision.

In our prayer for the Father's kingdom we celebrate its presence in our midst and we commit ourselves to work for its coming. Spoken with the Son and through the Holy Spirit, our prayer is a sacramental expression of the Father's kingdom.

Abba, *Pater*, Father, your kingdom come,
    a kingdom which
        reveals the life you share with us
        and shows the gentleness and power of your
            name.

We pray, Father, for your reign,
    knowing that it challenges ours
    and asks us to change.
We pray, Father, for your dominion,
    that we may express it as service
    in the company of your risen Son
    and empowered by the Holy Spirit.

Abba, *Pater*, Father, your kingdom come.
    May we welcome it in gratitude
    and work for it in fidelity,
    rejecting the allure of earthly kingdoms,

that through our efforts all may know
your reign of peace and justice in praying
Abba, Pater, Father, your kingdom come.

Eight

> Father,
> hallowed be your name.
> Your kingdom come.
> *Give us each day our daily bread*

In the first two petitions we turned to the Father and prayed for the fulfillment of our Christian vision:

> hallowed be your name.
>
> Your kingdom come.

With "Give us each day our daily bread," we pray for the fulfillment of our Christian mission.

As in the previous petitions we pray to the Father, but with a difference. No longer are we foreigners to the Lord's Prayer, outsiders asking to be taught how to pray. In the address we opened ourselves to our Father's life-giving presence. In the first petition we communicated with him in the gift of his name. In the second we accepted his loving dominion. The petition for our daily bread is the prayer of Christians who already share the Son's relationship to the Father and his vision for the hallowing of the name and the coming of the kingdom.

The third petition is longer and more complex than those which preceded it. But then the mission itself, with its many historical and social ramifications, is more involved than the vision which energizes and governs it.

The Greek text of the third petition has a unique and very striking word order which disappears in the English translation. Whereas all the other petitions begin with the verb or a conjunction followed by the verb, this central petition opens with a definite article and a noun, a direct object of the verb "give":

> hallowed be . . .
> come . . .
> *the bread (ton arton)* . . .
> and forgive . . .
> and do not bring . . .

The shift from the word order of the first two petitions alerts us to the beginning of a new series of petitions. The contrast with all the other petitions draws attention to the petition's emphasis on "the bread." The main concern in this petition is with *what* we ask the Father to give us and not with the need that he *give* it to us.

After the object, the petition continues with a possessive pronoun, "our." Its position after the noun is normal in Greek. However, after this pronoun we have a second definite article and the adjective *epiousios*, which is normally translated "daily," but which we shall have to examine more closely. Literally, the first part of the petition thus reads:

> the bread our the *epiousios*

The ordinary Greek construction for this would have been

> the *epiousios* bread our

which in our English word order becomes

> *our epiousios bread*

By repeating the article and placing *epiousios* after the pronoun, the Greek text clearly means to emphasize *epiousios* as well as "the bread." The petition's concern is not with just any bread, but with the bread which is *epiousios.*

After "our bread, the *epiousios*," we have the verb "give," an imperative form as in "hallowed be" and "come," but in the active voice. The verb is followed by an indirect object, literally, "to us," and another direct object, literally, "the each day," a very compressed expression for "the bread of each day." The second part of the petition, "give us the (bread of) each day," parallels the first clause of the next petition, "forgive us our sins" and has all the simplicity of the other three petitions.

In the third petition, we thus pray that the Father give us

our bread,
the *epiousios* (bread),
the (bread of) each day.

These multiple references to the bread leave no doubt that it must have been very special and the object of extraordinary reflection when the prayer was first formed.

In both Matthew and Luke the first part of the petition, "our daily bread," is identical in every respect, and we may safely assume that it comes to us unchanged from the prayer's oldest traditional form. Beginning with the verb, however, the Matthean and Lukan traditions differ significantly. In Matthew, the Greek verb "give" refers to a single act, and the indirect object "to us" is followed by the adverb "today." In Luke, "give" is in the present, a tense which connotes repeated giving and which is required by the object "the each day." In this case Matthew is very likely the one who preserved the oldest form.

When the prayer proved inadequate for a new situation, the Matthean community simply added further elements at the end of the section, as it did in the address and the petitions for the vision, and as it would do at the end of the mission petitions. It did not alter the wording that was already in place. Luke, on the other hand, preserved an adapted form which had become more suited to his communities' view of salvation history and the daily challenge of missionary commitment.

Our analysis of this third petition will first explore the meaning of bread, our daily bread, the bread of each day, and the Father's giving of such bread. As in the previous chapters, we shall then examine the dynamics of praying that the Father "give us each day our daily bread."

Meaning and Implications

The first of the three petitions associated with the Christian mission is extremely rich in meaning. The implications of the word "bread" become clear from other passages in Luke's gospel when these are placed in their cultural context. The word for "daily," a neologism, yields its meaning when we ask why the Christians coined a new word to describe their bread. The expression "each day" has an Old Testament background which shows why this bread must be given by the Father.

Bread, Food and Meals

Bread. The word is deceptively simple. Everyone knows what bread is. The Greeks, and the New Testament, called it *artos.*

In Lukan language, as indeed in the entire New Testament, the term referred first of all to little flat loaves, very much like those which we call Lebanese or Syrian bread. These loaves were usually made of wheat, but they also could be made of barley. In this sense bread is a food, a very ordinary physical reality which serves as human nourishment. This is the term's most basic meaning.

We find this usage, for example, in Luke 4:1-13, in the first of Jesus' three temptations. Jesus was in the desert, where he had been led by the Spirit. Having eaten nothing for 40 days, he was hungry. Since he was very hungry and had no bread, the devil suggested that surely as the Son of God he should command a stone to turn into bread. Now the Judean desert, which is not a sandy desert, is strewn with flat pieces of limestone, some of which look very much like loaves of bread. The devil either pointed to such a stone or held one up to Jesus. With most of us, in these same circumstances, the stone's size, shape and color surely would conjure up a loaf of bread, and our eyes immediately would start feasting on it. Not so with Jesus, who turned to scripture and told the devil that human life is not from bread alone.

In the context of the temptation bread refers directly and only to a loaf. In his rejection of that temptation, however, Jesus enlarges the term to mean food.

Bread is a food, one of many foods. The common Greek word for food in and out of the New Testament, was *trophe.*

For New Testament peoples bread was a staple food,

the primary staple. Normally three loaves sufficed for a meal.
No meal was without bread, just as in many parts of Asia no
meal is without rice. Can we imagine a good Italian meal
without pasta? an Irish meal without potatoes?

All other food was eaten with bread. Bite-sized pieces
could be torn from the flat loaf and dipped into a sauce, as
some accounts of the Last Supper imply (Mk 14:20; Mt
26:23). Americans eat potato chips in much the same way.
Mexicans dip tacos in guacamole. Bread was also eaten with
more substantive foods, such as fish or lamb. These could be
folded into the bread—the ancestor of the Near Eastern
felafel, the grand-ancestor of the sandwich. Fingers were the
basic utensil, and bread was their normal extension.

Little wonder that Jesus' response to the devil used
bread in the more general sense of food. In the New Testament bread often served as a designation for food, all food.
For example, in the shipwreck account in Acts Luke
repeatedly refers to food *(trophe)*, to taking food, and to
something to eat. However, the only specific food mentioned
is bread (Acts 27:21,33-38). We must not think that bread
was the only food available. As a general term it simply referred to all the food there was.

The two terms, "bread" and "food," were thus inter-
changeable. The use of the word bread as the equivalent of
food also underlies Luke's important theological expression
"the breaking of bread" (Lk 24:35;Acts 2:42,46;20:7-11).
Recall further how at the Last Supper, bread and the cup sufficed to designate the entire Passover supper (Lk 22:14-20).

An excellent point of reference for understanding this
usage is the expression "to have tea," which is widely
employed in much of the English-speaking world. It refers to
the entire evening meal, which might even substitute coffee
for tea. Even so, the meal is called tea, and no one is bothered
by the anomaly. Or again, some Chinese greet one another in
the morning with, "Have you had rice yet?" Having rice corresponds to our having breakfast.

Some of our modern languages still use the word bread
in an extended sense. The French, for example, refer to *casser
la croute*, literally, "to break the crust." Etymologically, our

English word "companion" means someone who has bread with another. In its Old French and Latin origins it surely referred to all the food taken and not merely to bread.

With several Lukan passages we have seen how bread referred more generally to food. In each case, however, except perhaps for Luke 4:1-13, we also sensed that it went beyond food. All the examples called for a further word, "meal."

In the human context of the New Testament bread and food are rarely dissociated from meals. As with us today, there were many kinds of meals. The main meal, supper or dinner, was called *deipnon*. This is the word used in the expression "Lord's Supper" (1 Cor 11:20). The noon meal or lunch was called *ariston*. Both of these could be festive, but the ordinary word for a banquet was *doche*. "Eating bread" was a common expression to refer to any or all of the three—supper, lunch and banquet.

In Luke-Acts "bread" consequently referred to more than just food, especially when accompanied by verbs such as "eating," "breaking" and "giving." It referred to a meal, whether ordinary or extraordinary. Besides the daily meals there were sabbath meals, Passover meals, and the meals which Christians shared on the first day of the week. All of these, including the ordinary meals, could be extremely meaningful in the person-oriented cultures of the New Testament world.

Loaves of bread and food are to a meal what walls, ceilings and floors are to a home. These structural elements are essential, but of themselves they constitute only a house, not a home. It takes people, relationships and the sharing of life to make them a home. Likewise, food is essential, but of itself it serves only a biological function, as in the case of animals, whose eating is called feeding. It takes people, communication and sharing to turn feeding into a meal.

Luke's gospel is especially rich in meal accounts. Together they help us to see how bread and food have human significance and how they acquire their full natural meaning in a human context. They also help us to see their social significance, how they fulfill their natural purpose in the context of sharing.

In the New Testament bread refers to a particular food, a loaf; to food in general; and to a human meal. As a child of his time and culture, Luke used the term in all three ways.

We are now in a much better position to understand our petition for bread as formulated in Luke. As the Lukan context shows, bread includes all food and sees this food in the human and social context of meals. A good translation for the petition would then be, "Give us each day our daily meal." The meal includes food, and obviously bread, but it also includes the human relationships of those who gather to share the meal.

With this realization, however, we have only begun to discern the implications of "our daily bread." We still have not come to grips with what Jesus meant when he said that life is not of bread alone.

For Jesus, as Luke presents him, bread, food and meals have a profoundly religious dimension which transforms and shapes their human reality and makes them a sign or symbol of the gospel. They thus have a place in the life and mission of Jesus' followers and are directly related to their vision that their Father's name be holy and his kingdom come.

Our Daily Bread

The translation "our daily bread" comes to us from late second-century translations of the New Testament into Latin and their use in the Latin liturgy. So venerable and accepted is this ancient translation that even today, in spite of its problems, it stands unquestioned except in scholarly circles. My purpose is not to question it, but to reflect on it in light of its Greek original, *epiousios*.

The word *epiousios* appears for the first time in the Greek text of the Lord's Prayer. The word never appears in ancient literary Greek, in the popular Greek of the papyri, which approximates the spoken language, elsewhere in the

New Testament, or even in subsequent Christian literature save in references to the Lord's Prayer.[1]

To decipher the meaning of *epiousios* scholars ancient and modern have examined it philologically and tried to unravel its secret by exploring its component elements. Somehow *epiousios* must have something to do with being and substance. But how and what? Others have searched translations in other ancient languages such as Syriac, Coptic, Ethiopic and Armenian, only to find a bewildering variety of renderings. In some of these translations, "our daily bread" is even "the bread for tomorrow."

These two approaches, which have sought to establish the word's meaning and have failed to yield conclusive results, may be too limited. Would it not be better to start by asking the obvious question: Why would the earliest Christians have coined a new word to describe "our bread"? The question leads us away from the question of meaning to that of purpose, a question prior to that of meaning.

The answer is obvious. As with every neologism, the community came forward with a new word because existing language proved inadequate. For this to be the case, *"our bread" had to represent a new experience of meal which was uniquely Christian.*

With this conclusion as our starting point, it then becomes possible to indicate what "our daily bread" referred to. In this further step, however, the word's definition is quite secondary. What is important is its association with significant experiences of meal. Apart from this association, the word has little or no meaning in the ordinary sense which can be established by a word's usage in multiple contexts.

Along with their abstractive, defining function, words have an indicative function. In the case of *epiousios*, as with proper names, this indicative function is primary. *Epiousios* is a proper adjective. Like proper names, such as Simon

1. One possible exception has surfaced in an Egyptian papyrus, but the text is mutilated at the very word *epiousios*. Even if the conjecture that the few preserved letters do belong to the word *epiousios* were to prove correct, the papyrus is much later than that of our New Testament writings, let alone the early traditions of the Lord's Prayer.

Peter, Martha and Mary, which speak to us to the extent that
we know the person to whom they refer, *epiousios* is significant only to the extent that we enjoy experiential knowledge
of the Christian meal.

The pronoun "our" in "our daily bread" helps to identify the meals to which *epiousios* refers. But what does "our"
mean in this context? The word is a possessive pronoun, but it
would make little sense to ask the Father for the bread which
we already possess. It could refer to the bread which we can
rightfully claim as sons and daughters of the Father. Use of
the possessive pronoun would thus spring from the rights and
expectations inherent in such a relationship. Used in conjunction with the new word *epiousios*, however, it must mean
more than this. "*Our* bread" refers to the bread or meal
which is characteristic of us as Christians, and this meal can
only refer to one which is taken with Jesus, the Christ and our
Lord.

Luke's gospel presents several accounts of meals with
Jesus. Taken together they describe what Luke saw and
understood in the expression "our daily bread." The Christian meal is first of all a call to discipleship and a reconciling
event (5:27-32;7:36-50). The meal also shows how Christians
are sent on mission (9:10-17), how they are to welcome one
another in hospitality on their Christian journey to the
Father (10:38-42), how they are to relate to one another and
share with the poor (14:1-14;16:19-31) and how they are to
celebrate the return of a Christian who was lost or dead but
who is now found and alive (15:1-32). The meal expresses the
gift of one's life for the life of others (22:14-38). In it Christians recognize their risen Lord (24:13-35). Need we search
any further to know why human beings do not live by bread
alone?

In very early times, which antedate St. Paul's letters,
the characteristic meal of Christians came to be called the
Lord's Supper and the Table of the Lord (1 Cor 11:20;10:21).
For Luke it was "the breaking of bread" (Lk 24:35;Acts
2:42), an expression which brings out the profound sharing
aspect of meals with the Lord. The emergence of these names
for what would later be called Eucharist constitutes a plausi-

ble reason for the disappearance of the expression "our *epiousios* bread" outside of the Lord's Prayer. The descriptive names spelled out some of the reasons why the Christian meal was so special and *epiousios*. The adjective, which relied for its significance on a good experience of the meal, spoke very little in troubled contexts with little or no sharing, and not at all to those who had not yet experienced the Christian meal.

The Bread of Each Day, Gift of the Father
        The expression "each day" *(kath' ēmeran)* does not appear in Matthew's form of the petition, which asks that our Father give us *today* our daily bread (6:11). By requesting the bread of each day rather than the bread for today, the Lukan tradition shows great sensitivity to the demands of long-term history. That Luke resonated with that tradition's view of life in history is clear from his own repeated use of the expression "each day" in the gospel (9:23;16:19;19:47) as well as in Acts (2:46,47;3:2;16:5;17:11;19:9). In nearly every case the expression appears in a general summary made by the Lukan narrator. Some describe the activities of Jesus (Lk 19:47), an early Christian community (Acts 2:46;17:11) or Paul (Acts 19:9). Some refer to the growth of the community (Acts 2:47; 16:5) or to the life situation of a particular historical figure encountered by the apostles (Acts 3:2).
        As summary statements these references demonstrate Luke's emphasis on continuity and development in Christian history. His use of the expression "each day" highlights one of the conditions required to maintain that continuity. Seen through Lukan lenses, the prayer for the bread of each day addresses a fundamental need of Christians living in history.
        Two of the summaries which include the expression "each day" take us beyond Luke's emphasis on Christianity's historical dimension and reveal some specific aspects and attitudes of Christian life in history. Like the petition for our bread of each day, both are attributed to Jesus.
        In Luke 9:23 Jesus asks his disciples to commit themselves to his way of life not just once but each day. Those who wish to be Jesus' disciples must deny their very selves, take up their cross *each day* and follow him. This summary of

the conditions for following Jesus was drawn from Mark 8:34. In Mark, however, Jesus makes no mention of "each day." Those who follow Jesus must make a radical commitment once and for all, an emphasis which remains unchanged in Matthew 16:24. By introducing "each day" Luke shows himself more conscious of the followers' need to renew their Christian commitment over and over again as they pursue the life journey which Jesus has already traced for them.

Luke 9:23, in which the author deliberately modified Mark 8:34 to include "each day," enables us to discern Luke's interpretation of "each day" in the tradition of the Lord's Prayer. The bread of each day is the bread of those who view life and history as a journey to the Father in the following of Jesus, whose death gave new meaning to the cross and transformed it into a symbol for Christian commitment. In the Last Supper account (22:1-38), Luke would show how the bread of each day responds to Jesus' farewell command that the disciples renew what he did at the Last Supper in remembrance of him. The petition for the bread of each day asks our Father for the gift to join Jesus in giving his person and pouring out his life for others. It also asks for the gift to join him at his table in the kingdom (22:28-30). The prayer for the bread which characterizes us and the bread of each day is thus intimately related to the vision of the Father's kingdom or reign for which we prayed in the second petition.

In our petition for bread, each day is a day in a historical journey through the passion to the Father. In 9:31 Luke presents that same journey's orientation as an exodus. Like that of the Old Testament, the Christian exodus begins with a Passover supper. Like the Israelites who were given a bread from heaven in the form of manna in the course of their exodus, those who join Jesus in his exodus also need a heavenly nourishment, a bread of each day just as the manna had been a bread of each day (Ex 16:4-5). The Christian manna, however, is not meant merely to sustain us on our journey but to nourish us in fulfilling the journey's purpose. *The Christian manna is a meal in which Christians give of themselves to the full and enter into Christ's glory.*

Only the Father can provide such bread, and he does

provide it to all who seek his kingdom. Anxious hoarding is therefore completely out of place on the Christian journey. All we need is the bread of each day, and this is the only bread for which we pray.

One of Jesus' parables (16:19-31) begins by describing a rich man who feasted sumptuously *each day* while a poor beggar lay starving at his door. Like 9:23, this usage of "each day" by Jesus helps us to discern the social and historical implications of our bread of each day. The parable focuses attention on what the Christian bread of each day must never be. The rich man's table was a selfish table, completely unmindful of the poor. It was the bread of one who sought to be served, not of one who served (22:24-27).

The bread of each day which our Father gives, on the other hand, is a bread which Christians generously share with one another and especially with the poor, each according to his or her need. This is the meal described in Luke's summary of life in the Jerusalem community in Acts 2:42-47. The same meal (14:12-14) inspired one of Luke's most memorable beatitudes: "Blessed is the one who eats bread in the kingdom of God" (14:15). Finally, this same meal, this breaking or sharing of bread, strengthens Christians when life is threatened, and brings them to salvation (Acts 27:21-44).

Dynamics

We have seen how the third petition presupposes those which look to the Christian vision, and how it addresses the most fundamental needs of the mission, all of which are related to our distinctive Christian meal, the bread of each day. In the first part of the chapter we have examined the meaning of the petition, how its elements are associated with Luke's view of history and the Christian journey to the Father.

As we did in previous chapters with regard to the address, "Father," the hallowing of his name and the coming of his kingdom, we shall now explore the dynamics of praying "give us each day our daily bread." It is not enough to understand the meaning of the petition. We must also understand what it means to pray it.

Give Us Each Day Our Daily Bread
There is a major difference between a petition which asks for the unfolding of our mission in history and petitions which ask for the ultimate fulfillment of our Christian vision concerning the Father's name and kingdom. In praying that the Father's name be hallowed and his kingdom come, we become attuned to that vision by praying for its realization. The Father's name is actually hallowed and his kingdom comes in the very act of prayer. Through prayer the seed which has been planted grows toward its full maturation. The same is true of our addressing God as Father. As, through prayer, we grow in the life of the Father, he becomes more and more Father to us. Our prayer is answered even as we pray it, and to the extent that we pray it as we ought.

While this is true for the first part of the prayer which establishes our relationship to the Father and to the ultimate goals which draw us forward in our mission, it does not always obtain in a petition which addresses the needs of the mission. Such a petition does indeed dispose us to undertake the mission and to join in a sharing meal which looks beyond history to the kingdom's full deployment. However, the petition is answered only as we engage in the mission and to the extent that the mission expresses in act what we prayed for in word. We know what it means to pray this petition only when it is answered, just as a blind person knows the meaning of a prayer for sight only when sight is actually granted.

To know what it means to pray, "Give us each day our daily bread," we must do what we pray for and join in a meal which is characterized by the attitudes represented in our discussion of "our *epiousios* bread" and "the (bread of) each day." As in the following of Christ and Christian liberation, knowledge is inseparable from praxis. We may know a few things about the following of Christ as outside observers, but we can never really know what it means to follow him without doing so. How could anyone know the meaning of liberation without being liberated and without engaging in the liberation of others? We may know something about "our daily bread" without experiencing it in a sharing meal, but we come to know what it really means only by giving and receiving it in a meal which manifests our solidarity with others and demonstrates our life commitment. We know what it means to pray for our daily bread when that prayer is answered in Christian praxis, that is, in what Luke calls the breaking of bread.

How then can Luke make the general statement, "to one who knocks it is opened" (11:10)? Jesus' statement does not say that it will be opened later when you break bread, but that it is opened even as one knocks. Does this statement apply only to the first part of the Lord's Prayer and not to the second?

The dilemma vanishes when we recognize that the Lord's Prayer was intimately associated with the Lord's Supper in early Christian tradition. The early Christians prayed the Lord's Prayer while gathered for the Lord's Supper, and many of its themes express those of the Lord's Supper. When prayed within the supper, the prayer helps us to see how the supper itself is a prayer, a prayer of thanksgiving in which we gratefully acknowledge that the Father answers our prayer and gives us the very bread for which we pray as we offer it to others. What seemed to be an exception to Luke's view of how prayer is answered in the act of prayer remains so only when the Lord's Prayer is dissociated from the supper which expresses it in gesture, symbol and act, as well as word. For the supper to do this authentically, however, it must not be an act isolated from the rest of life, but an expression of what Christians do and commit themselves to do outside of the sacramental breaking of bread. Otherwise it becomes a sacramental sign of nothing, an illusory sign void of symbol, a prayer which speaks to no one, a non-prayer which empties the Lord's Prayer of meaning and frustrates the mission.

With the Son, Through the Holy Spirit

We pray for our daily bread with the Son who has already entered fully into the Father's dominion. We pray it at the Lord's earthly table which sacramentally mirrors and actualizes his festive meal in the Father's kingdom (Lk 22:14-20). We pray it as men and women who have received the Son's promise of a place and role in the Father's kingdom (22:29-30).

Our prayer is effective and our meal is our very special meal, a meal which epitomizes the Christian mission, not because it is ours but because it is the Lord's. In the Lord's Supper, the Son joins us as a participant and transforms our relationships and attitudes. Like the disciples at Emmaus, we recognize the risen Lord and experience him at prayer when we reach out to those who have been strangers to us and invite them to our table. In that gesture our table becomes the Lord's table.

Jesus is no longer present to us as a historical figure. Our experience of him at prayer is consequently different from that of the disciple who originally asked that the Lord teach his disciples how to pray. However, Jesus is sacramentally present to us as Lord in the breaking of bread, and we can experience him at prayer like the Lukan communities which recognized the Lord in those they welcomed in hospitality.

We meet the Lord at prayer in the very meal for which we pray. There is no question but that the Father is ready to give us this meal. The Lukan tradition did not find it necessary to insist that he give it. Like the disciples of Emmaus, however, it is possible not to recognize the Lord who is present to us and blindly to pour out our grief to the one present as though he were absent.

The Lukan prayer emphasizes our need for a particular kind and experience of meal, one in which we meet and recognize the Lord, witness his prayer and are moved to ask that he teach us how to pray. He does so as we join him in his great eucharistic prayer and offer our lives for the salvation of others as he once offered his. To know whether our Christian meal is celebrated as it should be, we need only ask whether it reflects the relationships and attitudes of sons and daughters gathered at the table of the Son, whose whole life showed us how we are to live and act.

The principle of the Father's life in us is the Father's own creative and energizing Spirit which the risen Lord brings to our table. The same Spirit through whom Jesus was conceived, who descended on him at his baptism and who inspired his mission, descended on the apostles at Pentecost and on all who were baptized by them. Unlike John's baptism, which was in water alone, Jesus' baptism is in fire and Spirit, the fire and Spirit of Pentecost.

It is through the Holy Spirit then that we were baptized in Jesus' name and became sons and daughters of the Father. As in the apostolic community, the Holy Spirit overflows into all our relationships, enabling us to teach as the apostles taught, to join together in fellowship or *koinonia,* to share in the breaking of bread and to address our needs to the Father in prayer (Acts 2:42). To pray the Lord's Prayer as sons and daughters with the Son, we must therefore fan the flames of the Spirit which has already been given to us. We do so primarily at the Lord's table. Each celebration of Eucharist manifests the Father's gift of the Holy Spirit, attunes us to the life of the Son, opens us to his prayer experience, makes us receptive to his teaching, and enables us to pray as he did.

Conclusion and Prayer

The third petition in the Lord's Prayer, "Give us each day our daily bread," introduces our concerns for life in the Christian mission. We ask for the bread which is characteristically Christian, a manna for our Christian exodus, a meal in which we share as Jesus shared, the memorial of his Passover. Each time we celebrate this meal as a Lord's supper or breaking of bread, we move closer to our Christian vision that the Father's name be hallowed and his reign established.

When we pray for our daily bread in the context of the Eucharist, we place ourselves at the Lord's service and recognize his presence in our midst. And our prayer is fulfilled. Spoken with the Son and through the Holy Spirit, our prayer proclaims the blessedness of all who eat bread in the kingdom of God.

> *Abba, Pater,* Father, give us each day our daily
>   bread,
>   the Christian bread in which
>   we share your life,
>   glorify your name
>   and manifest the generosity of your
>   kingdom.

> We pray, Father, for a bread broken and shared,
>   a bread which
>   strikes at our selfishness
>   and opens our table to all your children.
> We pray, Father, for our exodus meal,
>   a manna which
>   strengthens us in our journey
>   and which we share along the way
>   as heirs to your Son's Spirit
>   and stewards of his table.

> *Abba, Pater,* Father, give us each day our daily
>   bread.
>   Open our hands wide to receive it
>   and open them wider to share it,
>   that in our breaking of bread
>   all may know what it means to pray
>   *Abba, Pater,* Father, give us each day our daily
>   bread.

Nine

Father,
hallowed be your name.
Your kingdom come.
Give us each day our daily bread;
and forgive us our sins
even as we ourselves forgive
everyone who is indebted to us

The petition for our daily bread is the first of three which concern the Christian mission. The second of these, "and forgive us our sins even as we ourselves forgive everyone who is indebted to us," deals with reconciliation, a facet of the mission which is very closely related to the breaking of bread.

In the previous petition we asked for a meal which invites all people to discipleship, unites us in the fellowship or *koinonia* of the Father's Son, gifts us with the Holy Spirit, and sends us on mission. By joining in that meal we actually hallowed the Father's name and made his kingdom present in our midst in a sacramental way. We thus contributed to the fulfillment of the Christian vision and committed ourselves to the reality which we now celebrate and proclaim in sacrament.

In this second mission petition we focus on reconciling forgiveness, one of the meal's principal functions. Our petition for forgiveness is thus implicitly contained in the petition for daily bread, just as the petition for the coming of the Father's kingdom was implied in the request that his name be hallowed. In the first mission petition, we focused on the positive things which we need to realize our mission. We asked for the meal which our Father gives to those who humbly pray, and for all the good things which spring from it. We prayed for the peace of the Lord's new covenant. In

129

the second mission petition we show awareness of our sinfulness, of the evil which separates us from our Father and
from those who want to share in his life. We ask that the
meal's eucharistic peace overcome our disunity and heal our
personal and social wounds.

The petition for forgiveness is by far the longest and
the most complex of all the petitions in the Lord's Prayer.
Both Matthew and Luke express it in two related clauses: the
first addresses our need to be forgiven by the Father; the second our need to forgive others. In both gospels the Father's
act of forgiveness is contingent in some way on our forgiving
others.

Differences between the two gospels in the petition's
wording and meaning are many. The first clause, which is
grammatically linked to the previous petition by the conjunction "and" opens with a verb in the imperative, "forgive,"
whose subject is "Father" (Luke) or "our Father in heaven"
(Matthew). The verb is followed by a pronoun indicating
those who are to be forgiven, "us," and a direct object
denoting what is to be forgiven, "sins" (Luke) and "debts"
(Matthew), both of which are modified by the pronoun
"our."

Differences in the second clause are even greater. In
Matthew our forgiving is referred to as a past act. Within the
petition, the fact that we have forgiven our own debtors provides a comparative basis for our Father's forgiving us our
debts. In Luke our forgiving is referred to in the present as an
act which coincides with the Father's forgiving us. The act in
which we ourselves forgive others is thus presented as a
sacramental expression of the act in which the Father
forgives us. In addition to this major functional difference,
we note that Matthew refers to those who are our debtors,
while Luke speaks of those who are indebted to us. Using a
participle form of the verb, the Lukan text focuses directly on
the active relationship between those who are indebted and
those to whom they are indebted rather than on the person of
the debtors. Finally, Luke's use of the universal "*everyone
who is indebted to us*" in lieu of Matthew's simple "our debt-

ors" corresponds to his tradition's sensitivity to the gospel's universal invitation to salvation.

It is safe to assume that Matthew's form of the petition, "and forgive us our debts, just as we forgave our debtors," represents the older of the two traditions. As we indicated earlier, the Matthean community retained the wording which had been handed down to it. When modifications were considered necessary, they were made by adding new elements at the end of the prayer's various units. The Lukan tradition, on the other hand, altered the wording to fit its context and theology. In the present case this required breaking the primitive parallelism between "forgive our debts" and "forgave our debtors."

Our analysis of Luke's fourth petition begins by examining the meaning of its terms as defined by their Lukan context. Going beyond this effort to understand the petition, we shall then explore the dynamics of praying it.

Meaning and Implications

The many differences between Luke's form of the petition and that of Matthew indicate that the area of sin and forgiveness was more open to a variety of theological interpretations than other areas covered by the Lord's Prayer, and that differing interpretations had an immediate effect on the petition's wording. We must consequently examine the terms "sin" and "debt," the meaning of forgiveness, and the relationship of the Father's act of forgiving to ours. As with the petition for bread, the analysis requires close attention to the New Testament and Lukan cultural contexts.

Sins and Debts

The first clause in Luke's petition for forgiveness uses the word "sin" *(hamartia)*, a theological term, in place of Matthew's "debt," a term originally associated with economic life but whose meaning could easily be extended to other kinds of relationships. The second clause uses the expression "everyone who is indebted" in place of Matthew's "debtors." Both of these changes are theologically significant. To grasp their meaning, we need first to explore the notion of debt and indebtedness in the New Testament context.

In New Testament usage, the words "debt" *(opheilēma)*, "to be in debt" *(opheilō)* and "debtor" *(opheilētes)* refer to a variety of human situations which have a number of things in common. All result from the fact that someone has done something to or for someone else. All express a relationship of dependence between the parties concerned. And all require further action or behavior which flows from this relationship. Debts, however, are not all the same, and what distinguishes them is far more obvious than what they have in common. In the New Testament we find three distinct but closely related kinds of debts: debts of justice, debts of gratitude, and debts of offense. To appreciate the third category, the debts of offense, which is immediately relevant to the Lord's Prayer, we must situate it with regard to the other two.

Debts of justice are familiar to all of us, and the easiest to understand. For example, when someone works for an employer, the employer incurs a debt toward the employee. Until the debt is removed by the payment of wages, the employer is a debtor. Paul refers to this kind of debt when he contrasts gratuitous justification through faith with earned wages rightfully received in exchange for work. Such wages are not given as a favor or grace but owed as a debt (Rom 4:4). Or again, someone who buys goods from another without paying immediately or borrows something with the intention of returning it later also incurs a debt and that person's relationship to the one who sells or lends is that of a debtor. Jesus refers to such situations in parables; for example, he speaks of two men who owed money to a moneylender (Lk 7:41), and of a clever manager who decreased the debt which two debtors owed his master (Lk 16:5-7). In each case, the employer, buyer or borrower has incurred a debt which must be paid in justice. When the debt is paid, justice is served.

In debts of justice the primary focus is on what is owed, something quite objective and measurable. In Western cultures which do not emphasize the personal relationship between the parties, they can be completely paid. Once paid, the debt is no more. However, in other cultures, including New Testament cultures, a personal element is always present. The one who benefits from the transaction retains a debt of gratitude to the one who worked, sold or lent, even after the debt of justice has been removed. The debt of justice is transformed into a debt of gratitude.

Debts of gratitude are more complex than debts of justice. In Luke 16:5-7, for example, those who had their debt to the master reduced incurred a new and very different kind of debt to the manager. Acting within his discretionary powers, the manager gratuitously offered his master's debtors something which justice did not demand. In accepting it, they took on a debt of gratitude in his regard, a debt which altered their relationship to him and required that they see to his personal needs once he became unemployed. In Luke 7:42-43 the moneylender wrote off the debts of the two debtors who could not pay. Their debt of justice was removed, but they took on a new debt, one based on a favor graciously granted rather than on a contract mutually accepted. Repayment of this debt would be determined by the demands of gratitude, and not by those of justice. The same is true of Romans 4:1-8 where Paul speaks of reconciliation as a grace which God freely offered to Abraham. Accepting in faith a gift to which he had no right, he became indebted to God in gratitude.

In debts of gratitude the primary focus is not on something objective and measurable which of its nature can be repaid, but rather on the personal relationship between the parties. Debts of gratitude result from gifts freely given and freely accepted. They can never fully be repaid. A gift, however, does call for a response. When, for example, we say to someone, "I am deeply indebted to you, and I can never repay you for what you have done," we indicate that we shall do everything we can to repay even though full payment is impossible. When the gift is love and life, it calls for loving service and lifelong gratitude. When the gift is life in Christ, it can be repaid only with the gift of our own life. Need we wonder why we celebrate Christ's gift of himself in a Eucharist or thanksgiving, or why we celebrate it over and over again even though his gift was once for all? Throughout the New Testament, our relationship to Christ can be described as a debt of gratitude. As we pray the Lord's Prayer, we stand before our Father with an enormous debt of gratitude which we know we cannot repay, and we ask him for even more blessings which will increase that debt.

Debts of offense are even more complex than debts of gratitude. Such debts result from a personal affront and they call for repentance. Repentance alone, however, can never remove the debt. Debts of offense can only be absolved by the one who has been offended. Forgiveness is a gift. When the offended party extends a hand of peace and accepts the offender's repentance, the debt of offense is transformed into a debt of gratitude.

In cases where the offender already was bound by gratitude to the one offended, the debt of offense is far greater and calls for a far more generous act of forgiveness. When the one offended is our Father, who has freely given us life, manifested his name to us, given us a share in his kingdom and graced us at the table of the Lord, the debt of offense is immeasurable. Only he can forgive such a debt and transform it once again into a debt of gratitude. When we are offended in our relationship to others, we alone can offer forgiveness and bring about a reconciliation.

As children of the Father, Christians are reconcilers by definition. The Father is one who forgives, and Christians witness to his life in history by forgiving. Refusal to forgive strikes at their very identity as sons and daughters of the Father, rejects the Father's life and constitutes a new and abiding debt of offense toward him. Repentance for this debt is expressed in the forgiveness of our own debtors. Only then can we sincerely pray that our Father forgive us our debts (Mt 6:12).

The above analysis helps us to understand the terms "debts" and "debtors" in the Matthean tradition of the Lord's Prayer. It also helps us to grasp the relationship between one who is indebted and the one to whom he or she is indebted.

The Lukan tradition of the Lord's Prayer focuses directly on this personal relationship. Referring to "everyone who is indebted to us" rather than to "our debtors," Luke emphasizes the dynamic dependence and the interpersonal tension which calls for a forgiving release. His "everyone" calls attention to the universality of forgiveness. As in Jesus' encounter with a lawyer who wanted to distinguish those who were his neighbors from those who were not, we are reminded that *all* are our neighbor (Lk 10:25-37). Just as the lawyer's love could not be exclusive, neither can our forgiving gesture. There is no distinguishing those who are deserving of our loving forgiveness from those who are not. Christian forgiveness· must extend to everyone who is indebted to us, without concern for who they are.

In the first part of the petition the Lukan tradition substituted "sins" for "debts." It adapted the prayer's wording to developments in the synoptic tradition. The use of "debts" in Matthew 6:12 reflects an extremely early Christian usage which predates the synoptics. In that usage the same term was used to describe offenses against the Father and offenses among Christians and others. After its use in the earliest form of the Lord's Prayer, the term "debts" never again appears in New Testament references to offenses against God. Offenses against God, our Father, are designated as sins. The term *hamartia* ("sin") is thus a special theological term which expresses human offenses against God, offenses which disrupt the relationship of grateful sons and daughters to God their Father.

In John's and in Paul's letters, the word "sin" is often personalized and referred to in the singular as an inimical agent in history. In Mark, Matthew and Luke-Acts, however, we find it almost exclusively in the plural and in reference to human acts against God. Use of the plural reflects a Christian awareness that in our unique relationship with the Father we can and do offend many times and in many ways. In Luke-Acts and in the Lukan tradition of the Lord's Prayer, use of the plural, "sins," corresponds to Luke's emphasis on the continuity of Christian life in history with its need to take up one's cross daily and to be nourished each day with the Lord's manna. Like the Christian challenge and communal sharing in the breaking of bread, sin is not a one-time event but a repeated reality.

Forgiveness, Divine and Human
    In the New Testament the words "forgiveness" *(aphesis)* and "to forgive" *(aphiēmi)* are usually associated with sins, but not exclusively. The same Greek words can also refer to the freeing or release of prisoners; to someone's leaving, as when Peter and his partners left everything and followed Jesus; or to the act of permitting, as when Jesus permitted no one except Peter, James and John to accompany him into a home or when he asked that the little children be allowed to come to him. In each case the words refer to a situation of restraint or exclusion, and to its transformation into a situation of freedom and association. Together they help us to appreciate the meaning of forgiveness.
    To forgive is to free or release someone, to leave something behind, something which impedes a relationship, and to allow a relationship to be re-established. To forgive a debt is to release someone from its obligation and to introduce that person into a free relationship. To forgive people their sins is to free them from all they have done to mar or break their relationship to the Father.
    Western cultures tend to treat forgiveness quite lightly. The popular saying, "Forgive and forget," attests to that. Forgiveness is usually not difficult for us. That may be because our relationships are often superficial. We meet people easily. In a matter of minutes, it is as though we had known them all our lives. Once they go away, we forget them, and it is as though we had never known them.
    In most other cultures, however, forgiveness is extremely difficult. This is reflected in popular sayings such as "I forgive, but I can never forget" and "I forgive, but the wound runs deep." The difference between these cultures and ours lies in their great sensitivity to persons and personal relationships. Where every human relationship is significant, forgiveness is not taken lightly or granted casually.
    Forgiveness cannot be taken lightly because the rela-

tionship it wants to restore is not taken lightly, and the offense which wounded it is personal. The more personal the relationship, the deeper the affront. The deeper the affront, the more difficult the forgiveness. This is true of our own culture in special cases, usually among people related by family ties or longstanding friendship. In the more personalist cultures, it applies to most relationships, to the shopkeeper and his client, the beggar in the public place and the passerby who daily extends a coin, the waiter and those he serves, even to politicians and those whose trust they hold.

The cultural world of the New Testament was very personalistic. Those whom Jesus addressed consequently took offenses very seriously and forgave with great difficulty. We see this very clearly in the story of the prodigal son. The older brother refuses to forgive his younger brother; he even refuses to recognize him as his brother and refers to him quite pointedly as his father's son. "This son of yours," he says to his father. "This brother of yours," the father responds. We observe it also in Jesus' teaching to the disciples. When their brother does wrong, they must correct him. When he sins against them even seven times a day and repents seven times a day, they must forgive him that many times. In a context where forgiving even once was difficult, we can appreciate how demanding Jesus' ethic of reconciliation must have seemed to the apostles. "Increase our faith," they said. The Lord Jesus answered that they were being asked no more than their most basic duty as servants of reconciliation (Lk 17:3-10).

Against this cultural background which viewed forgiveness as very difficult, we can only wonder in astonishment at Jesus' prayer of forgiveness on the cross: "Father, forgive them. They do not know what they are doing" (Lk 23:34), and at Stephen's prayer which echoes that of Jesus, "Lord, do not hold them accountable for this sin" (Acts 7:60). We can also appreciate the change of heart which enabled the disciples to pray "and forgive us our sins even as we ourselves forgive everyone who is indebted to us."

The cultural attitudes which made it difficult to forgive also made it difficult to ask for forgiveness. In a per-

sonalist culture, asking to be forgiven is humbling. The
Pharisee in one of Jesus' parables could not bring himself to
do so. Instead he proclaimed his personal dignity, sinlessness
and righteousness. A tax collector, on the other hand, from
whom no one expected humility, prayed very simply,
acknowledging that he was a sinner and begging God's mercy. When Jesus says that those who exalt themselves shall be
humbled while those who humble themselves shall be exalted, he is addressing the cultural tendency to find great
value in personal aggrandizement, display, social prestige
and being honored. He accepts the value of honor and indicates its true source. There is no escaping humility. The
choice is between humbling oneself and being humbled by
God. The first leads to true honor. The second brings shame
(Lk 18:9-14).

The same saying concerning exalting and humbling
oneself concludes Jesus' brief discourse to the guests at a dinner in the house of a leading Pharisee, a public figure. All
were seeking places of honor at the table, places close to their
important host. Jesus raises the possibility that a personage
greater than they might arrive, that they might have to cede
their place and proceed in shame to the lowest place. Is it not
preferable to take a lowly place and be invited higher?
Humility is the price of honor. Shame is the cost of self-
aggrandizement.

Aware of these values, we can now appreciate the initiative of one of the criminals dying on a cross next to Jesus.
His humble request for forgiveness would lead to exaltation
with Jesus in the kingdom. The other criminal's defiant
refusal to ask forgiveness leaves him dying in shame on the
cross.

It is just as difficult to ask for forgiveness as to forgive.
In our reconciliation petition we take on both challenges. We
ask the Father to forgive us, and we proclaim our forgiveness
of others. The more sensitive we are to the personal relationship between the Father and ourselves and between ourselves
and others, the more we appreciate what is required of us in
praying the petition and the more noble our request. Joining

Mary, the blessed one, in her lowliness, we shall surely be exalted (Lk 1:48).

The forgiveness for which we pray is divine. Addressing God as Father we appeal to the Father's love for us and count on his willingness and eagerness to forgive, an expectation well-portrayed in Jesus' story of the father who ran out to welcome his repentant son. When the son acknowledges his personal unworthiness to be called son, the father ignores his declaration, restores him to his honored place in the family, and celebrates his return with a banquet (Lk 15:11-24). Again the humble is exalted.

Only the Father can forgive sins, offenses committed against him. As Jesus attests in Luke 10:22, however, everything has been given over to the Son by the Father. The Son thus acts in the Father's name and extends his fatherly forgiveness to sinners. In his ministry, Jesus' forgiveness of sins caused no little consternation. Once, while curing a paralyzed man he said, "Your sins are forgiven," instead of, "Be cured, arise and walk, through your faith you are healed." The scribes and Pharisees immediately questioned Jesus' authority. Jesus must be blaspheming. God alone could forgive sins. In his response Jesus shows that physical healing is but a sign of a deeper healing, one which cures spiritual wounds in a person's relationship to the Father. Healed of his paralysis, the man can now walk in the way of the Lord (Lk 5:6-26).

Later, when Jesus tells a repentant woman whose love is great that her sins are forgiven, some of those present echo the question of the scribes and Pharisees, "Who is he that he even forgives sins?" (Lk 7:47-49). Neither the scribes and Pharisees in Luke 5:6-26 nor the dinner guests in Luke 7:47-49 recognize that Jesus is the Son of Man, *the* human being, and that in being Son of Man he is also the Son of God. They fail to see that, as the Son, Jesus is able to express the Father's love and extend his merciful forgiveness.

In Jesus, the Son of Man and the Son of God, forgiveness is both divine and human. All who share in his sonship, all to whom he has effectively revealed the Father, to whom he has given the dominion which the Father had given to him, and who preach repentance and heal in his name extend that forgiveness to others. Like that of the Son, our forgiveness of others is divine and human. In forgiving everyone who is indebted to us, we forgive as sons and daughters of the Father. We give human expression to the Father's divine forgiveness. The norm of Christian compassion and forgiveness is consequently the Father's own compassion and readiness to forgive (Lk 6:36).

With the Father's own compassion as our norm, a compassion which far exceeds that of an ordinary human parent, we do not judge or condemn those who are indebted to us. We forgive them, and in doing so we are forgiven by our Father, not judged or condemned. In forgiving, we are forgiven; the more generously we forgive, the more totally we are forgiven.

Such is the meaning of the fourth petition in the Lord's Prayer. Our forgiveness of others is a sign of repentance for our own sins. We ask the Father to grace that sign by forgiving us our sins. Forgiven in the very instant we forgive, our act of forgiveness extends the Father's forgiveness to everyone who is indebted to us.

Dynamics

In the first part of this chapter we examined the meaning of "debt," the different kinds of debts and how they are interrelated. We also looked at the meaning of "sin," a theological term which replaced Matthew's "debts" in the Lukan form of the prayer. Then we studied the notion of forgiveness and saw how difficult it is to forgive and to ask forgiveness when personal relationships matter deeply. Finally, we showed how the Father's forgiveness becomes incarnate in that of Jesus his Son and continues to be sacramentally communicated through the forgiving acts of those who share in his sonship.

We shall now explore the dynamics of praying "and forgive us our sins even as we ourselves forgive everyone who is indebted to us." We want to know what it means to pray this petition, not merely what the petition means.

And Forgive Us Our Sins

Jesus' whole mission can be summed up in the words salvation, liberation and reconciliation. In his preaching, teaching, healing and exorcising, as well as in the sacrificial offering of his passion-resurrection, he offered salvation from death, liberation from sin, and reconciliation to the Father. The forgiveness of sins for which we pray opens us to all three aspects of his mission. It speaks our eagerness to accept his offering for ourselves and to pursue his mission on behalf of others. By forgiving everyone who is indebted to us, we offer his salvation, liberation and reconciliation to a new period of history. Forgiveness is coextensive with the Christian mission.

In our prayer we ask to be forgiven in the very moment we pray, and it is in that same moment that we forgive everyone who is indebted to us. In this respect the prayer for forgiveness is like the petitions that the Father's name be hallowed and that his kingdom come, both of which are answered in the act of praying. In praying for forgiveness, we are forgiven. The prayer is therefore a special sacramental act, an act of the church speaking mutual forgiveness, and requesting forgiveness for its sins against the Father, an effective act in which all who pray are forgiven even as they forgive.

At the same time the prayer recognizes the recurrence, plurality and pervasiveness of sin in human life. Sin is a daily offense which affects all our relationships. It must consequently be forgiven regularly and in life's many contexts. Were we to seek forgiveness only in the privileged context of prayer, our prayer for forgiveness would become ineffective, a promise easily made and rarely fulfilled. Forgiveness must reach out of the prayer into daily living. In this respect the prayer for forgiveness is like the petition for the bread of each day, which is answered in our sharing meal, as well as in all the sharing which flows from it and takes place outside of the meal.

In praying for forgiveness we commit ourselves to Christ's mission of forgiveness, and we expect our prayer to be answered wherever and whenever we engage in that mission. Our prayer is answered when we pray it in the assembly for the breaking of bread, a reconciling meal in which the Lord's Prayer is fully at home.

Jesus' story of the prodigal son shows how the breaking of bread, our Eucharist, celebrates the sinner's return. The father welcomes his younger son who had strayed in death but was now alive, who had been lost and was now found. He also pleads with his older, unforgiving son to join in the celebration. The father illustrates both parts of the petition, the way our prayer for forgiveness is answered and the way we are to forgive others. The younger brother models the humble attitude which as sinners we must have in approaching the Father and in joining him in the banquet. The older brother mirrors the difficulties we have in forgiving and in joining our repentant brother in the banquet. In praying the Lord's Prayer at Eucharist, we are the younger son who was lost and is now found and the older brother who must overcome all resistance to forgive (Lk 15:11-32).

Outside the meal, in the marketplace, at the factory, in the lecture hall, in the boardroom, at the office and in the home, in all the places where we sin, the Lord's Prayer rises from our hearts and springs to our lips. The simple invocation, "Father," is often enough to evoke the whole prayer and its eucharistic commitment to forgive. In saying "Father" as unworthy sons and daughters, we reach out to our brothers and sisters. We forgive and we are forgiven.

Spoken from the heart the prayer for forgiveness is a transforming prayer, helping us to recognize our sinfulness, to set aside our pride and to overcome our inner resistance to forgive. Every time we pray it, we grow as a reconciled and reconciling people. The Lord's Prayer and its petition for divine and human forgiveness spurs us to conversion, a gradual and lifelong process. Challenged and prodded by the prayer we utter, we undergo a change of heart or *metanoia* which will one day allow us to speak our final act of forgiveness. Having taken up our cross, we shall forgive like Jesus on his cross forgave and be ushered into the eternal banquet of the Father's kingdom.

With the Son, Through the Holy Spirit

Of ourselves and through our own power there is no way we could meet the demands of Christian forgiveness. Praying like the proud Pharisee we would remain locked in our pride, holding ourselves better than the tax collectors and sinners of the modern world. Unforgiving like the older son, we would refuse to recognize our brother in the Father's younger son. Judgmental like the Pharisees, we would protest the presence of sinners at meals with Jesus.

With the Son and through the Holy Spirit, however, we can forgive everyone who is indebted to us and find forgiveness for ourselves. We do so in the breaking of bread, a reconciling table, which is not just our table but the table of the Lord.

The Lord is present at our Christian table. He is present in the persons of those who participate at that table. Through the power of the Holy Spirit he extends forgiveness to all sinners through their act of forgiveness, making it the Son's forgiveness. He is present in the bread and wine which we share. Through the power of the Holy Spirit he reconciles all those who give and receive that bread and wine in remembrance of him. He forgives others and we are forgiven in the gift of his body and blood.

In union with the Son we humbly pray for forgiveness. Like the tax collector of Jesus' parable, we are forgiven. In union with the Son, who is our brother, we join all our brothers and sisters in the banquet of reconciliation. Unlike the older brother in Jesus' parable, we overcome our jealous and resentful feelings. In union with the Son, who offered his life for the forgiveness of sins, we offer our own lives that those who were dead might live. Unlike the Pharisees, we offer peace and solidarity to all who accept the Lord's gracious presence.

Through the Holy Spirit, the Father's creative Spirit, we transcend our human limitations. We learn to forget as we forgive, not out of indifference or shallowness in our relationships, but as the Father's children, as men and women who value their brothers and sisters and are sensitive to them.

We also overcome our feelings of shame, and we humbly ask for forgiveness, knowing that we shall be exalted by the Father's forgiving love.

With the Son and through the Holy Spirit our debts of offense, our sins, are transformed into debts of gratitude, debts we can never repay any more than we can ever repay the gift of life. We accept the Father's forgiveness, a gift freely given. We offer this gift to others and build up a community of gratitude, a eucharistic community bound to the Father in thanksgiving.

Praying with the Son, the Father surely gives us the Holy Spirit, empowering us to forgive not only the few who form our intimate circle but all who have been walking blindly without faith or who stumble lamely in the way of the Lord. With the Son and through the Holy Spirit we prepare a people reconciled, ready to greet the Lord at his coming.

Conclusion and Prayer

In our petition for daily bread, the bread of each day, we asked the Father for a sharing meal in which we transcend all human selfishness, reach out to the poor, the lame and the blind, and contribute to the coming of the kingdom. In this first mission petition we asked to recognize the kingdom which already is in our midst. We asked to manifest the kingdom's presence so clearly that all who join us at the Lord's table exult in Luke's beatitude: Blessed and happy are those who eat bread in the kingdom of God.

In the second mission petition we focused on an important aspect of that meal, reconciliation among ourselves and with God our Father. We asked to be forgiven all our sins against the Father, everything which we have done to distort his image in us, to detract from his kingdom and to reduce the Lord's table to our own selfish table. We asked to be forgiven in the very act of our forgiving everyone who is indebted to us. We asked to be forgiven above all for our failure to forgive, to welcome sinners to our table and to join our repentant brothers and sisters at the Lord's table.

> *Abba, Pater,* Father, forgive us our sins,
>> forgive us our sins
>>> even as we ourselves forgive
>>> everyone who is indebted to us.

> Forgive us, Father,
>> that your name be hallowed
>> and your kingdom come.
> Forgive us, Father,
>> that we may extend your forgiving hand to
>> others,
>> that with your Son and through the Holy Spirit
>> we may welcome those who are indebted to us
>> to your reconciling table.

> *Abba, Pater,* Father, forgive us our sins.
>> So may we always pray,
>> humbly, trustingly, perseveringly,
>> overcoming our resistance to ask forgiveness
>> and our reluctance to grant it,
>> and inviting all to join us in praying
>> *Abba, Pater,* Father, forgive us our sins.

Ten

Father,
hallowed be your name.
Your kingdom come.
Give us each day our daily bread;
and forgive us our sins
    even as we ourselves forgive
    everyone who is indebted to us;
and do not bring us to the test

The petition that our Father not bring us to the test is the third devoted to the Christian mission and the concluding petition of the Lord's Prayer. In the petitions for the hallowing of the name and the coming of the kingdom we fixed our gaze on the horizon of life and history. We focused on the Christian vision which draws us forward as we journey in the way of the Lord. In the petitions for the gift of daily bread and fatherly forgiveness we directed our gaze to the whole course of life in history. We focused on the Christian mission and on all we need to fulfill it as we reach for the vision in which the Father's name is hallowed and his kingdom fully manifest.

In our final petition we look to the decisive moment, the climax of our missionary journey, a climactic moment which is also the threshold of our entry into glory and the fulfillment of our vision. We focus on what we need, personally and as a church, to cross the Christian journey's bridge from life in history to the fullness of life in the Father's kingdom.

The petition is very simply worded, "and do not bring us to the test." After the conjunction "and," which links it to the previous mission petitions, we have the verb "bring" in the Greek subjunctive mode and with a negative, "do not bring." This verb, whose subject is "Father," has a direct object, "us." It is qualified by a prepositional phrase, "to the test" *(eis peirasmon)*, literally "to," indicating motion and direction, and "test," the term of that motion, the moment and situation in which we are supremely tested.

The subjunctive "bring" is the only subjunctive in the Lord's Prayer. In each of the four previous petitions, "Father" was the subject of an imperative. In English and many other languages, this subjunctive is almost impossible to translate clearly. When we render it by "do not bring," the difference between the subjunctive and the imperative is completely veiled and we tend to read the verb as an imperative. As a result we miss a crucial difference between this petition and the four which precede it.

The subjunctive is weaker and less direct than the imperative. It expresses a certain dependence either on someone's will, prayer or wish, or on some condition which will result in an action. When we say, "My prayer is that the Lord *be* with you and that you *be* well," the verb "be" in our prayer is in the subjunctive mode. Or again, when we refer to Jesus' saying to Mary and Joseph that it is necessary that he *be* with his Father, we express that necessity in the subjunctive mode.

In our petition, the subjunctive "bring" expresses a similar dependence or subordination. It subjects what we request to the Father's will, a will which is not directly expressed but which is implied in the address, "Father," and the role which "Father" plays as the subject of the verbs in the mission petitions, including this one. In Matthew this subordination is also expressed in the petition, "Your will be done," a petition not included in Luke.

The fifth petition is also the only negatively worded request in the Lord's Prayer. This negative, however, must be seen in the context of the subjunctive verb, which subordinates our negative request to the positive condition that the Father's will be done. A negative imperative would have indicated our will that something *not* be done. A negative subjunctive indicates our positive submission to the Father's will even as we express our negative request.

Up to the word "test," with which Luke's petition

ends, Luke and Matthew are identical in every detail of this petition. We have no reason to doubt that this clause, "and do not bring us to the test," constituted the original petition in its entirety and in its precise wording. Later, the Matthean tradition supplemented the negative request with a positive interpretation: "and deliver us from the evil one." For Matthew and his community, not to be brought to the test meant to be delivered from the evil one. Our Father certainly would not want us to be delivered to the evil one. In Matthew's addition we recognize this and accept his saving will. Again Matthew's more ample and more explicit form of the prayer helps us to understand the implications of the subjunctive and negative in "do not bring."

As with the previous petitions we shall begin by exploring the meaning of the petition. In the second part of the chapter we shall reflect on what it means to pray it.

Meaning and Implications

The noun "test" *(peirasmos)* and its verb "to test" *(peirazo)* are open to a wide variety of usages. Just about every aspect of human life can be tested. There are, for example, tests of physical strength and prowess, intellectual ability, and moral courage or stamina. There are also tests of authenticity and tests of commitment. In all of these a challenge is presented and we must prove our ability, worth or values.

Some tests are taken on willingly, as when we join in a race or match problem-solving ability with another person. Some tests are imposed, and in those cases we speak of being subjected or put to a test. The test referred to in the Lord's Prayer is one to which we could be subjected and one which we do not seek.

In every case a test must be seen as such in order to be a test. Otherwise it remains but a difficulty, a painful experience which should be avoided if possible. When a difficult challenge cannot be avoided, it can be transformed into a positive and enriching experience simply by viewing it as a test.

Every test has two aspects. It reveals or demonstrates

something which was unknown and which we want to know. By vigorously exercising our ability and drawing us to new levels of performance, it is a source of development and improvement. As such, the test is beneficial and can be sought without fear. But a test can also be too demanding. If it requires more than we can do, it is destructive and harmful. We can be overwhelmed by a test, and it is out of this awareness that we pray "Do not bring us to the test."

The Test

The test referred to in the Lord's Prayer is no ordinary test. The petition implies that this test is a matter of concern to the Father, and that he can preserve us from it. Its context in the Lord's Prayer indicates that it has something to do with the hallowing of the Father's name and the coming of his kingdom, and that it is related to our sharing meal and Christian forgiveness. Like the two preceding petitions, it involves the Christian mission and the mission's relationship to our Christian vision. The test is thus a challenge to the whole meaning and purpose of Christian life in history.

We can best discern the nature of the test, and grasp the petition's meaning, from the accounts of Jesus' prayer at Gethsemane. In Mark 14:32-42 we find Jesus filled with fear and distress and speaking his anguish to three of his disciples. In his sorrow he prays, "*Abba* (Father), all power is yours, take this cup away from me, but let it be not as I will but as you will." Then interrupting his prayer, Jesus returns to the three disciples, only to find them asleep. It is then that he says to Peter, "Be watchful and pray that you not be put to the test." Jesus then resumes his own prayer, using the same words as before. Jesus' prayer frames his warning to the disciples and tells us how it must be understood.

In his *Abba* prayer Jesus is actually asking the Father not to bring him to the test. His prayer tells us what it means for the disciples to pray that they not be brought to the test. Jesus' test is the passion, and its image at Gethsemane is the cup, a cup to which he had already referred in a dialogue with James and John (Mk 10:35-45). When the disciples asked to sit at his right and at his left once he had entered into his glory, Jesus asked if they could drink the cup he would drink and be baptized in the same bath of pain as he. To their response that they could, Jesus announced that they would. Later at the Last Supper Jesus offered them that cup, they took it, and all drank from it. That cup was the cup of his blood, the covenant blood, which would be poured out on behalf of many, a cup which he would not drink again until he drank it new in the kingdom (Mk 14:23-25). Now at Gethsemane, his prayer indicates that no one should seek the passion's test. The spirit may be willing, but the flesh is weak. The disciples could not even stay awake as he prayed. At the same time, the disciples, like himself, must be willing to accept the test if that should be the Father's will.

Luke drew his account of Jesus' prayer at Gethsemane (22:39-46) from Mark, but he rewrote his source in such a way that its relationship to the Lord's Prayer is unmistakable. Addressing the Father, Jesus drops the term *Abba* and retains only *Patēr* (Father) as we find it in the address of the Lord's Prayer. His command that the disciples pray so as not to enter the test receives more emphasis than in Mark. Instead of Jesus praying twice, he twice warns his disciples to pray, once at the beginning of the passage and once at the end. In Luke, Jesus' warning thus frames the body of the passage, and Luke is even more effective than Mark in showing the relationship between the disciples' need to pray and Jesus' prayer.

In Luke, as in Mark, the cup of Gethsemane evokes the cup of the Last Supper, the eucharistic cup in which the disciples joined Jesus in the commitment to pour out their lives on behalf of others. The Passover cup's role in Luke 22 thus parallels the test's relationship to our daily bread, our exodus bread, and to the forgiveness of sins in the Lord's Prayer. In sharing our Christian meal and in our reconciliation, we declare our willingness to risk our lives as we pursue our Christian mission. In the petition that we not be brought to the test we recognize our weakness and ask that our commitment not be tested to the full unless this be our Father's will, a loving Father's will which will not allow us to be overwhelmed by the test.

If we should have to undergo the test and suffer the

passion, our prayer is that we shall be able to do so as Christ did and as Stephen did. We pray that we may see our passion as a test and that we may give our lives as they did, committing our spirit to the Father and asking that he forgive those who subjected us to this test.

In the gospels, the test of the passion is preceded by many other tests. At the end of Mark's prologue, for example, we read that Jesus was tested by Satan during his 40-day period of preparation for the mission (Mk 1:13). Twice Jesus was tested by the Pharisees. On one occasion they tested him by seeking from him a sign from heaven (8:11). Later they tested him again by trying to trip him over a matter of law (10:2). Conspiring with the Herodians, the Pharisees also tested Jesus' allegiance to the Roman government (12:15). In these instances from Mark, Jesus either rejected the test or rose to its challenge, transforming what had been planned as a test for him into a test for those who plotted against him. In the passion he again accepted the test, transforming a successful attempt on the life of the Son of Man into a gift of life for others. Turning death's defeat into victory, Jesus found life for himself and for all who believed in the gospel.

Luke's gospel has similar tests which help us to appreciate Jesus' supreme test and the test mentioned in the Lord's Prayer. As in Mark there are the tests of Jesus' preparatory days in the desert, an episode much developed from Mark's simple statement. After an introductory mention that Jesus was tested by the devil, Luke presents the three tests which are also familiar to us from Matthew (Lk 4:1-13; Mt 4:1-11). In these the devil tested Jesus' acceptance of his humanity and his submission to God. As in Mark, Jesus was also tested by the Pharisees, who demanded from him sign from heaven (Lk 11:16).

One passage in Luke refers directly to the testing of the Christians. It speaks of those who at first received the word of God with joy but in whom it did not develop deep roots, so that they believed only for a while. Such people fall away in the moment of testing (Lk 8:13). In the Lord's Prayer we pray that the word of God develop deep roots in us and that we not be brought to the test unless or until this is the case.

We pray that we too accept our humanity and our creaturely status before God our Father and not fall away whenever we are tested by circumstances or persons. We ask to be watchful and to pray in all life's tests that we might be prepared for its final test. We heed Jesus' warning to pray constantly for the strength to escape whatever may be in prospect and to stand secure before the Son of Man (Lk 21:5-36).

Dynamics

In the first part of this chapter we explored the meaning of "test" and saw how the test to which we refer in the Lord's Prayer is the test of the passion. We interpreted this test and what it means not to be brought to it through the petition's relationship to Jesus' prayer at Gethsemane, an excellent commentary on several elements in the Lord's Prayer. Jesus asks his disciples to pray that they not go into the test even as he prays that the cup of the passion be taken away from him should that be the Father's will. We saw also how all the lesser tests of life come to a climax in the supreme test when in reality we drink the cup, the cup which we now drink in sacrament at the Lord's table.

We shall now examine the dynamics of praying "and do not bring us to the test." As with the four previous petitions, it is not enough to know the meaning of the request. We must know what it means to pray it. Only then are we fully attuned to the Lord's intention in Luke 11:1-13. The Lord Jesus taught us more than a prayer. He taught us how to pray.

And Do Not Bring Us to the Test

When we pray that the Father not bring us to the test, we pray not to be subjected to the ultimate implications of our reconciling meal, the laying down of our lives for others. We pray in recognition of our human weakness. We pray in full realization that we are no better than Jesus' first disciples, heavy with sorrow and apt to sleep in Gethsemane's test. We pray also as disciples whom Jesus rouses from sleep and whom he asks to pray that they not be subjected to the test (Lk 22:45-46).

At the same time, we pray in acceptance of our Father's will, the will of one who assigned the kingdom to his Son, who in turn assigned it to us. To take part in the Father's kingdom we must stand loyally by him in his tests and serve as he did, offering our lives for the salvation of others. Only then will we eat and drink at his table in the kingdom (22:27-30).

When we pray in humble recognition of our weakness and in acceptance of the Father's will, we stand before the Father as creatures who accept our creaturely condition and our creator's dominion. In this twofold attitude our prayer is answered, and we have all we need to meet the test of the passion should it come. Any other prayer would be unrealistic and foolhardy. Like Peter we might declare ourselves ready to face imprisonment and death at the Lord's side (22:33) only to find ourselves denying all relationship to him when these are threatened. Should we do so, may we shed repentant tears as Peter did upon recalling the Lord's warning (22:54-62).

At issue in the test is our very humanity. Can we accept being children of Adam while being children of God? Jesus showed the way in the triple test which preceded his life ministry. After the genealogy which concluded with "son of Adam, son of God," the devil tests Jesus by asking him to do certain things "if you are the Son of God." Each time Jesus affirms that he is Son of God while being fully Son of Adam or Son of Man. As Son of Adam he is not nourished by bread alone, he does not exchange human kingdoms for the reign of God, and he most certainly does not test God (4:1-13).

Unlike Jesus, Adam and Eve turned away from their humanity and reached for God's divinity. Rejecting the most radical limitation of human life, mortality, they sought to be immortal like God. They refused to be subjects in the creator's kingdom and tried to exercise his dominion. In doing so they found servitude and death.

In praying not to be brought to the test, but according to the Father's will, we recognize our creaturely limitations and the Father's dominion. We respond to the original temptation and react to our sinful tendency to exalt our lives and to exercise God's dominion as though it were our own. We stand before the Father as children who hallow his name and welcome his kingdom.

The garden of Gethsemane is our answer to the garden of Eden. The Lord's table with its bread of life is our answer to Eden's table with its fruit of death. The test of the cross is our answer to the test of the serpent. Not seeking the test, but accepting it if it be our Father's will, we find life, not by grasping for it, but by giving it.

With the Son, Through the Holy Spirit

Who could presume to meet the test of life-through-death with human resources alone? Who could presume to meet the challenge of original sin and evil? Alone we could but ratify Adam's sin, making it our own and contributing to the presence of selfishness and evil in our world.

Only with the Son, whose life we share, can we claim victory over evil's dominion. We do so in baptism, when we unite with him in selfless commitment to others, in sharing the Father's life as he did. We do so also in the Eucharist, where the Son acts as Lord. Renewing his passion's commitment in and through us, the Lord transforms our gift into a Christian gift of life. Meeting the Father in and through the Son's gift, we speak an eternal debt of gratitude to the Father. We do so finally in the Lord's Prayer when, with the Lord at prayer, we pray as sons and daughters that the Father's will be done with regard to the supreme test of Christian life, the pouring out of life for the life of the world.

Like the Son we pray through the Holy Spirit. When Jesus went out to the desert, he went filled with the Holy Spirit, the Spirit of divine sonship which came upon him after his baptism by John. During 40 days he was led by that Spirit and during 40 days he was tested by the devil. Tested by the spirit of evil, he responded to the test through the Spirit of good.

In our Christian journey, we too go filled with the Holy Spirit, the Spirit of adoptive sonship, which came upon us at our baptism in Jesus' name. Led by the Spirit throughout life, we too are tested by the spirit of evil.

Through the Spirit, we are not overwhelmed and destroyed by those tests unless, like Ananias and Sapphira, we try to test the Spirit himself (Acts 5:9). We test the Spirit when we challenge him to ratify outwardly what we do not profess inwardly, leading others to think that we are acting according to the Spirit of generous self-giving when in fact we are acting according to the spirit of self-interest.

Through the Spirit of Pentecost, the creative Spirit which transforms us into a new people who knows no racial, class or ethnic differences, we meet the test of our human limitations, our fear of death and our exclusive tendencies. We accept our creaturehood and the Father's universal dominion. The same Spirit which enables us to pray *"Abba"* empowers us to pray "and do not bring us to the test."

Conclusion and Prayer

The fifth and final petition of the Lord's Prayer, "and do not bring us to the test," looks down the course of our missionary journey to its term, to the moment when we shall join the Father in the glory of his name and kingdom. It speaks our attitude and prayer with regard to the possibility that all our lesser tests in life might climax in a supreme test, and that all our individual acts of witnessing might call for the supreme witness of a passion like that of Jesus. Asking to be spared this final test, as Jesus did at Gethsemane, we join Jesus in his submission to the Father's will.

We pray this petition with the Son, who prays in us and allows others to experience his prayer through us, in our baptism, in our Eucharist, and whenever we turn to the Father in his name. We pray it also through the power of the Holy Spirit who enables us to accept our human weakness and proclaim our submission to the Father's dominion.

> *Abba, Pater,* Father, do not bring us to the test,
> the test of Christ's passion,
> a witness to life unto death.

Do not bring us, Father, to the supreme test.
   We know its risks;
   we know our weakness.
But, Father, let it be as you will,
   a Father's loving will,
   a Father who would not bring evil
   to his children in the Spirit.

Abba, Pater, Father, do not bring us to the test,
   but if it be your will that we suffer it,
   may we do so in the likeness of your Son,
   praying that the cup might be taken from us
   revealing your loving will on the cross,
   and inviting all to pray
   Abba, Pater, Father, do not bring us to the test.

Conclusion
and Prayer

Tertullian, an early Father of the Church from North Africa, spoke of the Lord's Prayer as a compendium of the entire gospel. In this he had no intention of distinguishing one gospel from another. For him the whole gospel event, as we find it in the New Testament's many works, was summed up in the Lord's Prayer.

Tertullian was right. As one of the gospel's most basic statements the Lord's Prayer gathers up all the gospel traditions, digests them and transforms them into a gospel prayer. Its enthusiastic reception at every period of church history and the reverence with which it is prayed by Christian peoples everywhere attest to its simplicity, depth and spiritual potency. The Lord's Prayer is *the* gospel prayer, one whose every word breathes with the Spirit of the new covenant. We stand in awe before this prayer knowing that however long we study it, ponder it, and pray it, we can never exhaust its gospel resource.

Every New Testament writing helps us to plumb the depths of the Lord's Prayer, and the prayer itself illumines every part of the New Testament. This process of mutual interpretation is especially true of the gospel of Matthew and of Luke-Acts, which include a traditional expression of the Lord's Prayer in their respective gospel syntheses. To understand the prayer as prayed by Matthew and Luke and their communities we must study the whole of their gospel narratives. To know what it means to pray it as they did we must also live and love the gospel as they did. Reciprocally, to understand and live their gospel we must understand and pray their Lord's Prayer.

In Luke we saw how the Lord's Prayer was conceived by the Holy Spirit in those who experienced the Lord at prayer. Now that we have studied the meaning of the prayer and what it means to pray it, we have some sense of what the disciples experienced when one of them asked: "Lord, teach us to pray." Having felt our own inadequacy in understanding and in praying the prayer, we also know why as disciples of Jesus, followers of Christ and forerunners of the Lord, they needed to be taught how to pray. The prayer gave words to their experience and filled their helplessness with Christian self-understanding.

For so influential a prayer, we need to be very precise in its translation. The Lord's Prayer shapes our Christian identity and forms our view of life in creation and history at every level of our being. Breathed into the deepest levels of subconscious life and alive in its memory, it touches and transforms the synthesizing core of our Christian existence. Every word then becomes important. We can control our translation and the words we take in, but we have only minimal control over how they influence us thereafter.

We also need to be sensitive to the prayer's structure and to the function of its address and petitions. The entire prayer addresses the Father. In the Lord's Prayer, the name and kingdom of God are the Father's name and kingdom. The prayer's first and second petitions sum up the Christian vision, a vision which will be fulfilled in glory but which influences the lives of all those who journey toward that glory. The third, fourth and fifth petitions address the needs of our Christian mission. We ask our Father to give us food for the journey, a sharing meal which welcomes all his children, a reconciling meal in which our sins are forgiven as we forgive others. We also look to the end of our mission and the threshold of glory and speak our commitment to the Father's will with regard to the supreme test of Christian life and witness.

Luke's purpose was to bring his readers to genuine insight concerning matters which had been fulfilled in their midst and which they already knew. With Luke as a guide, we wanted to learn to pray a prayer which has been handed down to us and which we have long recited. Luke-Acts helped us to understand its terms and phrases and their relationship to Christian experience as a whole.

We saw that the Lord's Prayer is an adult's prayer, the prayer of one who knows what it means to give life. It is as fathers and mothers, as parents, that we address the Father of all. The prayer's impact escapes us when we make it a child's prayer, the prayer of one who knows only what it means to receive life.

We saw also that the Lord's Prayer is a socially conscious and very realistic prayer. The name refers to the Father's personal revelation to all who know his Son, risen to be the Lord of all. It knows no social barriers. The kingdom refers to the transformation of all earthly kingdoms into one kingdom of justice and peace. It breaks down all social barriers. The bread for which we pray is a feast which gathers everyone, including the poor, the lame and the blind, at the table of God's kingdom. The forgiveness it pledges extends to everyone and knows no privilege. Its boundaries are those of the kingdom. Knowing our weakness, we ask not to be brought to the test of the passion. We ask this for ourselves personally and for the whole church. We do so, however, in submission to the Father's will. We distort the prayer whenever we reduce it to an individualistic and escapist prayer.

Understanding the prayer is not enough. The Lord taught us to pray it. We tried to do so with our limited experience of the Lord, our reluctance to give full sway to the Spirit, and our shallow appreciation of the Father's life in us. Over and over again we tried. Once again, let us pray.

Abba, Pater, Father,
    your Son taught us to pray,
        your Son and our brother.
    We thank you for his prayer.

We thank you for your Spirit,
for blessed Mary's *fiat*,
and for the Son you sent us,
that through his life and gospel
we all might come to know you
and learn to call you Father.

Abba, Pater, Father,
hear our thanks
and listen to our prayer.

Abba, Pater, Father,
we exult in your name,
your Father's name most holy,
your name made flesh in Jesus.
Hallowed be your name
in all your sons and daughters
with whom he chose to share it,
that one day we may sing
in the vision of your glory:
"Holy, holy is your name!"

Abba, Pater, Father,
hear our prayer
and listen to our hope.

Abba, Pater, Father
we rejoice in your kingdom,
a kingdom of justice,
the reign of Christ's peace.
Your kingdom come
for all your children
to whom he promised it,
that one day we may shout
in the fullness of life:
"The reign of God has come!"

Abba, Pater, Father
hear our hope
and listen to our need.

Abba, Pater, Father,
   we gather at your table,
      the table of the manger,
      a table for your flock.
  Give us each day the bread we need,
      bread broken to be shared,
      the bread of thanksgiving,
  that with joy we may proclaim:
      "Blessed who eat bread
      in the kingdom of God!"

        Abba, Pater, Father
          hear our need
          and listen to our cry.

Abba, Pater, Father,
   we celebrate your mercy,
      a Father's loving mercy,
      generous and life-giving.
  Forgive us our sins
      as we ourselves forgive
      those indebted to us,
  that every time we pray
      all may hear your gentle
      "Peace, peace be with you!"

        Abba, Pater, Father,
          hear our cry
          and listen to our trust.

Abba, Pater, Father
  we accept your will,
      a Father's saving will
      which sees us through the journey.
  Do not bring us to the test.
      Let this cup pass from us,
      but your will, not ours be done,
  that should the passion come our way
      our hearts might turn to you and say,
      "Father, in your hands I place my spirit."

Abba, Pater, Father,
hear our trust
and listen to our love,
that in our prayer
all may come to know
that you are truly
Abba, Pater, Father.

Appendix

Translating is always treacherous. In the prologue to *The Wisdom of Jesus the Son of Sirach* the translator, who was the author's grandson, says that "what was originally expressed in Hebrew does not have exactly the same sense when translated into another language." The same is true of what was originally expressed in Greek. While as translators we try to respect "every single stroke of a letter" of the prayer (see Lk 16:17), we may well join Ben Sirach's grandson and ask everyone "to read with good will and attention, and to be indulgent in cases where, despite our diligent labor in translating, we may seem to have rendered some phrases imperfectly" (Si, Prologue, *RSV*).

Comparing Translations
    A comparison of four major translations will enable us to see the text of the Lord's Prayer a little more sharply. It also shows how each translation is an interpretation. The Greek text can be rendered in various ways. This is not just a question of precision in language usage or of correct understanding. Words are closely tied to cultures and their use gathers an enormous number of connotations around them. There is often no true equivalent for these as we pass from one language to another. Translators must select the expressions which in their judgment best express the original

165

Greek wording. In doing this, translators also act as interpreters.

A comparison of different translations is a study of interpretations. Together the translations help us to appreciate the meaning, associations and potential of the Greek text. The exercise is consequently useful even for those who know Greek. For those who do not, it provides a way of circumventing the lack.

Revised Standard Version (RSV)

Father,
hallowed be thy name.
Thy kingdom come.
Give us each day
our daily bread;
and forgive us our sins,
for we ourselves forgive
every one who is indebted to us;
and lead us not
into temptation.

New American Bible (NAB)

Father,
hallowed be your name,
your kingdom come.
Give us each day
our daily bread.
Forgive us our sins
for we too forgive
all who do us wrong;
and subject us not
to the trial.

New English Bible (NEB)

Father,
thy name be hallowed;
thy kingdom come.
Give us each day
our daily bread.
And forgive us our sins
for we too forgive
all who have done us wrong.
And do not bring us
to the test.

Jerusalem Bible (JB)

Father,
may your name be held holy,
your kingdom come;
give us each day
our daily bread,
and forgive us our sins,
for we ourselves forgive
each one who is in debt to us.
And do not put us
to the test.

By placing the translations side by side, a number of things become immediately obvious. We note first of all the great variety in sentence structure, punctuation and the use of capitals. We also note that aside from "thy" *(RSV, NEB)* and "your" *(NAB, JB)*, and the omission of "and" before "forgive us our sins," all four translations are fundamentally identical through the first part of the request for forgiveness. The one exception is in "hallowed be thy (your) name" *(RSV, NAB)*, where the expressions "hallowed be" and "thy (your) name" are transposed in the *NEB* and the *JB*. The difference is not enormous, but what of "be held holy" in the *JB*, which contrasts with "hallowed be" *(RSV, NAB)* and "be hallowed" *(NEB)?* Is there a difference between the name being hallowed and being held holy? The *JB* translation seems to limit the request to the way we speak the name. For many of us it evokes the commandment "You shall not take the name of the Lord your God in vain" (Ex 20:7). Is that the meaning of the petition? The *JB*, however, does imply that we have a part to play in hallowing the name, and this is not easily sensed in the other translations.

Beginning with the second part of the prayer for forgiveness, the translations vary enormously. "For we *too* forgive" *(NAB, NEB)* includes an oblique reference to the Father's forgiving. We ask that he forgive, for we also forgive. "For we *ourselves* forgive" *(RSV, JB)* is quite different. It emphasizes the fact that we do indeed forgive. In a comparison of the Lukan and Matthean texts, the significance of this difference becomes apparent.

Whom do we forgive? "Every one" *(RSV)*, "all" *(NAB, NEB)*, "each one" *(JB)*. Some translations focus on the universal, all. In so doing, they emphasize the complete openness of the one who forgives. Others draw attention to the individual persons who make up the all. Their emphasis is on the object rather than on the subject of the verb "forgive" and on all the individual instances where forgiveness is granted.

Forgiveness is required only when there is something to be forgiven. How is this expressed? Every translation is different: "who is indebted to us" *(RSV)*, "who do us wrong" *(NAB)*, "who have done us wrong" *(NEB)*, "who is in debt to us" *(JB)*. Is it the same to be indebted, to be in debt, to do wrong, to have done wrong to someone? Nuances can be significant.

The translations of the concluding petition vary most

of all. First there is the verb, "and lead us not" *(RSV)*, "and subject us not" *(NAB)*, "and do not bring us" *(NEB)*, "and do not put us" *(JB)*, which is rendered in four very different ways. Then "into temptation" *(RSV)*, "to the trial" *(NAB)* and "to the test" *(NEB, JB)* follow. Can "temptation," "trial" and "test" be translations of the same Greek word?

Let us assume that no single translation can actually say all that is found in the Greek text and that each of the four translations we have compared is a good interpretation. We might then convey the meaning of the prayer, while staying close to its form as a prayer, by using parentheses.

With the *Revised Standard Version* as a base the Lord's Prayer would then read as follows:

Father,
hallowed be thy (your) name.
Thy (your) kingdom come.
Give us each day our daily bread;
and forgive us our sins,
for we ourselves (too) forgive
everyone (all, each one) who is indebted to us
    (do us wrong, have done us wrong, is in debt to us);
and lead us not (subject us not, do not bring us,
    do not put us)
into temptation (to the trial, to the test).

This composite translation is obviously too wordy, too preoccupied with explanation, and too heavy for prayer. A good prayer is simply worded, unself-conscious, direct and light. As a preparation for prayer, however, it does enrich the vocabulary of the prayer with associations and nuances which no single translation can adequately express.

The Greek Text

Our comparison of four major English translations raised many questions about the precise meaning of the text. Some of these can be answered by the original Greek text. A look at the Greek text also reveals a number of things which escape the English language altogether as well as a mysterious word which defies adequate translation in any language.

With regard to the use of "thy" or "your" which

modify "name" and "kingdom" in the early part of the prayer, the issue is quite simple. The word "Father" implies both respect and intimacy. The same qualities should carry over in other references to our Father. Does "your" *(NAB, JB)* do this better than "thy" *(NEB, RSV)*? In many cultures it most certainly does, and wherever this is the case, the use of "thy" runs counter to the intended meaning of the prayer.

In Greek, the petitions that the name be hallowed and the kingdom come both begin with the verb. The emphasis is not on the name and the kingdom. It is not that we want to distinguish the name and the kingdom from anything else which might be hallowed or which might come. Rather, the prayer contrasts being hallowed and coming with *not* being hallowed and *not* coming. The Greek word order thus indicates that the transposition from "hallowed be thy name" *(RSV, NAB)* to "thy name be hallowed" *(NEB)* should be avoided. In the petition for the kingdom, however, such a transposition is necessary due to the active form of the verb.

In the request for bread the Greek verb translated "give" is in the imperative as it is in English. The Greek use of the present, however, implies a *repeated* giving, a nuance which the present of the English verb does not easily convey. The Greek form of the verb fits the context which asks our Father to give the bread not once but each day.

Unlike the two earlier petitions, the Greek text places the word "bread" at the beginning of the clause. Emphasis is consequently on the bread rather than on the giving. We ask for our bread, a bread special to us. The text assumes that the Father does give, and it finds no reason to stress this.

A look at the Greek text places a large question mark over the word "daily" in "our daily bread." The Greek word *epiousios*, which we translate as "daily," is highly problematic. It could mean daily, but this is almost impossible to verify. Whatever its precise meaning, it certainly indicates that "our bread" is very special. The term is examined more closely in the chapter on the petition for bread. For the present, it suffices to note that "daily" and "each day" are not tautological.

In the Greek text the petition for forgiveness is joined

to the preceding petition by "and." The dropping of the conjunction in the *NAB* obscures the close link between the two petitions. The other translations, which retain the "and" are more faithful to the Greek text.

More than any other gospel Luke has a penchant for the word "all," in Greek *pas*. Depending on the context this word can also be translated by "every," "everyone." Unlike the English word "all," the Greek term has both a plural and a singular form, depending on what it modifies. In the Lord's Prayer "all" modifies a singular form of a participle. Staying close to the Greek text we should consequently read "every one who is" *(RSV)* and not "all who are." The text refers to every single person who forms part of the "all." By translating "all," we leave aside the petition's sensitivity to individual persons and cases. "Each one" *(JB)*, on the other hand, does not adequately convey the sense of universality. Greek has another word to express "each" or "each one."

The participle which the *RSV* translates by "who is indebted to" conveys an active relationship. We can consequently exclude "who is in debt to" *(JB)*. Further, the verb to which it belongs means "to owe" or "to be indebted to" and says something quite different from "doing wrong to." By translating "who do us wrong," we would emphasize the wrong that is done. The focus of the Greek expression, however, is not on what is done but on the persons who do it and on their relationship to us. The translation "who do us wrong" *(NAB)* should consequently be excluded. Finally, by translating "who have done us wrong" *(NEB)* we would also refer to a past act or acts. Since the participle expresses a present or contemporaneous relationship and does not imply in any way the result of a past act, we have a second reason to set this translation aside. The only translation which holds up to a close scrutiny of the Greek text, then, is "who is indebted to us" *(RSV)*.

The last petition, "and lead us not into temptation" *(RSV)*, has always been problematic. Are we implying that our Father could be responsible for leading us into temptation? Repelled by the seeming implications of the request, translators struggle for a clear translation which does not do violence to our Christian sensitivities.

The literal meaning of the verb is to "bring in" or "carry in." When its object is a person it refers to transporting or bearing that person, as when some men were looking for a way to *bring* a paralytic, whom they carried on a mat, *into* the presence of Jesus (Lk 5:18). It can also refer to forcefully dragging a person in, as when Jesus tells the disciples what to do when they are *brought into* synagogues, into the presence of rulers and authorities (Lk 12:11). In both instances the meaning is very physical, and those brought in are either helpless or resistant. But what does the verb mean when it has nothing to do with a place, such as a house or a synagogue, and when those brought in are neither helpless or physically resistant? What does it mean to be brought into temptation? And how can this be best expressed?

In both English and Greek the verb "to bring" with a preposition is also used in a figurative sense, as when we say that we bring someone to grief. Since the verb in Luke's Greek is used both in a literal and in a figurative sense, and since English is open to both possibilities, it appears preferable to retain the translation "bring to" *(NEB)*. Theological problems arising from Christian sensitivities should be dealt with by the commentary and not by the translation.

What is the meaning of "temptation," and is it a good rendering of the Greek word *peirasmos*? For an answer we must examine both the gospel context and the connotations of words like "temptation" *(RSV)*, "trial" *(NAB)* and "test" *(NEB, JB)*. *Peirasmos* by itself could be translated by all three.

In English usage "temptation" is associated with moral situations where something draws us to sin. It is usually described, at least partly, in terms of a psychological struggle. In the gospels, however, even when used in the plural (Lk 4:13), *peirasmos* refers to a major critical moment in which the whole meaning and purpose of someone's Christian life could be frustrated. An excellent example of such a critical moment, and the usage of *peirasmos*, appears in Jesus' warning to the disciples in the Garden of Gethsemane: "Pray that you may not enter into temptation" (Lk 22:40, *RSV*) and "Rise and pray that you may not enter into temptation" (22:46, *RSV*). This moment is best described in historical, not in psychological terms. Since the connotations of "temptation" do not easily fit this context, we should look for another word.

The word "trial" is a possibility, but here again ordinary usage includes unacceptable connotations. In Christian spirituality we often refer to "trials," challenges which we repeatedly encounter along life's journey. The Greek word *peirasmos*, however, refers to something definitive, a climactic moment associated with Christ's passion and death. Outside of Christian spirituality the word "trial" views the one who is tried as passive. A trial is something to which we are subjected. What we need, however, is a word which expresses a definitive inner confrontation with a challenge which comes from outside us. For these reasons the term "trial" is best avoided.

The most acceptable translation seems to be "test," although it too has certain limitations. Unlike "trial," however, "test" always implies a personal challenge and effort to pass the test which is presented to us. In English the article, "*the* test," helps us to realize that this test is a supreme test, a definitive crisis through which we must emerge victorious.

A New Translation

From the above considerations, along with a careful comparison of the Matthean and Lukan texts (Chapter Four), the following translation would seem to most closely approximate the Lord's Prayer of the Lukan tradition:

> Father,
> hallowed be your name.
> Your kingdom come.
> Give us each day our daily bread;
> and forgive us our sins
>> even as we ourselves forgive
>> everyone who is indebted to us;
> and do not bring us to the test.